RIDING THE DARK HORSE

AND THE FALL OF MAN

LAMA NICHOLAS PACKARD

BALBOA
PRESS

A DIVISION OF HAY HOUSE

Balboa Press books may be ordered through booksellers or by contacting:

Balboa Press
A Division of Hay House
1663 Liberty Drive
Bloomington, IN 47403
www.balboapress.com
1 (877) 407-4847

Print information available on the last page.

ISBN: 978-1-5043-8840-5 (sc)
ISBN: 978-1-5043-8842-9 (hc)
ISBN: 978-1-5043-8841-2 (e)

Library of Congress Control Number: 2017914521

Balboa Press rev. date: 09/28/2017

"To my mother and father;
they deserved so much more."

There is in reality neither truth nor error, neither yes or no, nor any distinction whatsoever, since all— including contrariness—is one.

—Chuang Tzu

CONTENTS

Part III—Man Separates from Self

FOREWORD

By Jay Ramsay

Poet, Healer, and Psychotherapist, London and Stroud, UK

Nicholas Packard has a mind like a crystal. He is a man who is aligned in every cell of his being. Why? Because he's done the work of mastery over many years by studying with masters (in China and India) and doing the practice—most recently pioneering the use of qigong for health. His naturally philosophical and academically trained mind is, as a result, connected to the whole of life—the way philosophy originally was. And he has an important message for us now in our state of disconnection (from the body, the planet, and so each other) and distortion, vulnerable as we are in a disembodied state to darker astral and alien energies, that we have to return to what matters—to the higher self and to love, but also to our true embodied nature as human beings. We risk being or becoming nonhuman otherwise.

Our dystopian situation is reflected in newspapers every day. The spread of what Paul Levy calls *wetiko* (after the Native American Indians) or "bad virus" suggests definitively what we are up against with extremism and collective psychosis. And this is the dark before the dawn that the Book of Revelation enshrines: the end of the Kali Yuga likewise leaves us with having to integrate our own shadows, no longer simply as beings of light. But it is more than that. We have to reconnect to a vision of ourselves as *part* of divinity and *part* of the mind and will of God. It is our only healing, Nicholas would say (as Daskalos, the great Cypriot healer, also did before him), and this fine book tells us why. Life has a serious purpose after all: we are here for reasons we have mostly forgotten, and this is what we have to reawaken to. As the psychic Lyndsey Mackenzie put it to me, "Either the pattern dies, or you die." In either case the dominance of the ego—the *dark horse*—has to die and be transformed. It is ultimately a question of spiritual law. As another Scottish friend, the poet Alan Jackson, came to realize, "Shape up or you'll be removed." *The Dark Horse and the Fall of Man* is a huge and timely reminder. The line has been drawn. This is the time.

June 2017
Stroud, Gloucestershire, UK

PREFACE

My mother went to the hospital for a very simple procedure. She had the best doctors, the best hospital, and the best care that money could buy. Sadly, she died of an unrelated infection not long after the procedure. I was stunned and confused. I asked myself, "How did this happen? It doesn't make sense. The operation was a success, so how did she die?" I grappled for answers.

I can remember going into the bathroom after her death, looking in the mirror, and saying to myself, "Something is not right here; something is very wrong." Then I looked back at the perplexed image in the mirror and made a vow to it, saying, "If it takes me until the day I die, I will come to understand how this happened, and why—and find an alternative."

This book is in part a response to that vow, a journey to understand why Western medicine is failing, why the world is getting sicker and sicker—dying of cancer, and chronic and incurable diseases—and how America has become a nation filled with pill-popping, addicted, and depressed people. It is also an analysis on how the world has lost its soul, and perhaps most importantly, how our chronic, incurable illnesses (cancer) and our soullessness are connected.

I first went to India to seek answers, then to China, Tibet, Bhutan, and other areas of the Far East. I studied under great gurus and masters and trained in the ancient Eastern methods of holistic healing, which integrates mind, body, soul, and nature. In the meantime, I continued to analyze and ask, "What has gone wrong in the West?"

As I lived in spiritual lands, and as I observed the world around me in nonspiritual places, I could see how we've been separated from just about everything that is nonmaterial in life, and how, instead, we've become prisoners of materialism, duality, and artificiality.

Then it came to me; I realized that was it. That was the major cause of illness! We had become too materialistic! We are living our lives soullessly, outside of any spiritual, integrated, and holistic perception of reality. And we are doing that because we are living outside of nature, its rhythms and cycles, and without any connections to the sacredness of life.

In coming to understand the root cause of our illness as the lack of a natural, holistic, and spiritual-based understanding of reality—and also observing the progression and unfortunate proliferation of this man-made, materialistic perception of reality worldwide—I realized we've been hoodwinked! Basically, we've been totally conditioned to see reality only insofar as the Western perception of truth and reality permits, in materialistic terms.

Sadly, however, few people understand this truth because the entire world has been conquered by the Western mentality and its way of thinking. Nowhere in the world, no country has been spared the tentacles of the paradigm of the West; we are all fish swimming in the same waters, and as such, we cannot really see how this is all wrong.

As I learned to do healing work, and do it continually day after day, I witnessed the extraordinary results—results that defied human reason. I came to be convinced that this lack of holistic and spiritual understanding was the major cause of illness in the West and the rest of the world.

Over time I began to realize that maybe the assumption that illness only comes from a material cause was the problem. Perhaps our illness comes to us not because of a pathogen that has invaded our body but because of the weather, or the food, or our emotions, or from evil spirits. Indeed, perhaps it comes to us because we are not spiritual!

So I attempted to look at the origin of the way we think today, not just in terms of its flaws but also in terms of how wrong it is because of our failed assumptions. In any philosophical query, one must question the assumptions. We haven't done that in Western medicine. We've never questioned the assumptions of the cause of disease; nor have we questioned the assumptions made for most of our secular beliefs.

When I started questioning the assumptions, it opened up a big can of worms, and I started to see where everything was all wrong. It was all wrong because we're identifying the cause of illness as only a material-based cause; we are not seeing things holistically in terms of connections and interdependence.

We're not seeing things in terms of their spiritual unmanifest reality; we are only looking at the manifest material reality. It's wrong because we are not looking at the big picture, only at the individual parts. It's wrong because it's exclusive, not inclusive. Basically, it's wrong because we are only using the left side of the brain.

Every day I deal with people who are supposed to be dying, but they get better. How is this possible? How can qi, energy, or spirit make them better? How can my hands do something Western medicine cannot? How can I explain the reasons for this to people I heal? They do not understand what *holism* means; they have never heard of *qi* or *yin* and *yang*. They do not understand about an unmanifest reality, or spirit consciousness, or essences, or even how the weather is making them sick!

How can I explain that there are many causes of illness, but the most important cause is the mind? How can I help them to understand that they are responsible for their own diseases? Rain does not come when the skies are blue; likewise, illness does not come to us unless the conditions are right for illness. If they don't understand this, how can I ask them to change and heal themselves?

The Dark Horse is an attempt to help people understand how, over time, we were led down a dark path, how we lost our essence, how our spirit was taken out of us, and how we separated from nature and its sacredness. Basically this book explains how we have been conditioned to ride through time on a dark horse, a horse propelled by greed, desire, egoism, and a reality limited to the material world. It also explains how we can turn things around, too, by seeing things differently and riding on the white horse.

Perhaps, after we come to understand that our perception of reality is wrong—and we begin to awaken to and reconnect to the spirit and its natural and sacred ways—we can come to take responsibility for our lives again and to heal on our own. Then, just perhaps, so many people won't be dying of cancer anymore, or living life with so many incurable and chronic illnesses, or needing to take so many meds just to get through the day.

And perhaps, people will not have to look on helplessly as a loved one dies in their arms of a simple infection, or of a broken spirit.

Lama Nicholas Packard

INTRODUCTION

From the time of Descartes up until the present, Western humanity has been seeking to separate from the earth and gain absolute freedom and control over its environment and its natural dependencies, and in the process, attempting to win dominion over nature, over others, and over its self.

As people in the West have pursued this freedom from and control over their environment unflinchingly, they have gradually come to see themselves as independent of the living systems that support and surround them. And they have adopted a misguided belief that they can either ignore these systems or dominate and exploit them without any adverse effects to their world and to their long-term health and survival. Modern humanity—not to mention our planet—has been placed at risk by this egocentric belief in the individual's centrality and importance, as well as his or her separation, self-sufficiency, and autonomy from nature. With this illusory and myopic mind-set, human beings are self-destructing, and they are destroying their own nest in the process, which is a sure sign that they have become unhealthy.

Basically, modern humanity has become unhealthy because it is acting unnaturally, and it is acting unnaturally because it has separated from heaven, from nature, and from its self.

This separation began when people in the West started to lose a connection to their roots and an overall purpose and meaning in life, as mirrored in nature. And it was cemented when they moved out of the countryside and lost respect for the environment and started acting independently of their earthly and heavenly roots, no longer in harmony and in rhythm with natures cycles and patterns.

It began when people turned their back to heaven, to mystery, and to the spirit world, turning instead toward the world of knowledge and facts that can be seen and proven empirically. And it was solidified when they separated from a state of unity and oneness and started "humanizing" nature, outside and independent of it.

It began with human curiosity, and it was finalized with human arrogance—when they believed that man-made creations, ideas, and values were true representations of life and reality and not simply products of their own invention. It was set in stone when they created an inflexible mentality of opposing dualities: heaven and earth, body and soul, good and evil, right and wrong, mine and yours.

From this time onward, Westerners refused to live a natural life in terms of essences, purpose, and organizing principles; they were not willing to live life as it comes to them naturally and spontaneously.

Rather, humankind has become more interested in controlling life, not in living it according to the laws of nature but in living outside of those laws—in ways determined by humans and invented by humans, and in ways they can manipulate and control.

In this way, humanity focuses on discovering the previous causes of material things and people and jettisons the purpose and final causes from the equation. In the process, it determines that things have to be seen and tested to be true. So people set down rules of investigation, which prevent them from being active participants in what they are investigating.

Hence people are expected to be separate from or outside of what they are examining and separate from nature and their nature. In this way, it is no longer necessary to know the essences of things and their purpose but more important to know the physical laws and structures of the universe—chemical, biological, molecular, atomic, and genetic. For all intents and purposes, the immaterial and unmanifest come to be ignored as significant principles of life and reality. As a result, life comes to be defined in terms of its material properties, which can only be identified as *real* when they have been observed and tested repeatedly to be true.

Thus, the soul and its purpose—its connectivity and its reason for being here—become irrelevant, an unnecessary component in the investigation of phenomena and things. Indeed, the less the soul is involved in examining the nature of reality, the better.

So the "invisible" purpose for which things exist, and which keeps the world in balance—previously explained as the cause of the organizing principle of life, the soul/spirit—is no longer admissible. It is no longer relevant, either. Instead, reality comes to be defined in terms of its material properties and how they can be measured objectively.

Nowadays our world is largely defined in these terms—in terms of science and materialism, in terms of causality and reason, in terms of knowledge and intellect, in terms of artificiality and duality, in terms of freedom and individuality, and in terms of objectivity and logic.

These qualities not only shape our belief systems, our values, and our ideals, but they also impact our perceptions of truth and reality, as well as our perceptions of right and wrong. Basically, they condition the way we think, the way we act, and the way we see and approach life.

Most people are unaware of this conditioning and the way these forces are influencing us today because, first of all, most people are unaware that they have been conditioned in the first place. Secondly, they are unaware that there is another way of thinking and interpreting reality. Indeed, not since the West conquered the world and imposed its version of truth and reality on the people of the world—in terms of its philosophy; its religion; its form of governance; its political, economic, and educational systems; its standing armies; its scientific truths; its health-care models; and its focus on commerce, trade, materialism, freedom, art, and modernity—has there been another cultural paradigm to follow.

Because of the omnipresence of the paradigm of the West and its preoccupation and identification with materialistic, physical, and artificial needs, modern humanity has over time lost the connection with its natural instincts and spiritual roots. In the process, individuals have lost the connection to nature, heaven, and their self in all their mystery and wonder.

Herein lies the fundamental problem. Fish cannot see outside of the waters where they swim. Likewise, modern humanity cannot see outside the waters of its cultural conditioning, since the same culture has influenced every place on earth. As there is no other way of living our lives, there is also no other way of seeing reality; there is only one way, the way that has been established and decreed by the West and its culture.

Thus, the spirit and wisdom, hitherto believed to be the reason for our existence and purpose (our essence, so to speak)—as well as the source of our intuition and virtues and the bridge between the manifest and unmanifest (this world and the other world)—has become obsolete, even inadmissible, as far as modern humanity and the paradigm of the West is concerned.

As a result, people in the West have come to lose their identity as spiritual entities, and being here has lost any meaning and purpose. They no longer see a connection to a world above and a soul within. Instead, life has come to be defined by its mechanistic laws, and man-made interpretations have replaced a natural reality.

Without feeling connected to either the world above or the soul within, they have come to think only in terms of what is below, in this material world, and have lost themselves in self-indulgence and pleasure. The ego and fulfilling its desires has become the object of people's lives. Thus, humanity's essential goal in life has been wiped out by desire and a reasoning intellect. Everything has come to be reduced to material causes and effects.

As a result, people no longer live in unity and harmony with nature, respectful of their environment, others, and their self. They have lost this spirit of balance, gratitude, appreciation, modesty, humility, and love. As a consequence, an improper way of life, and lifestyle, has emerged, and it has reached its fullest expression because of the influence of the paradigm of the West.

This mentality, with its symptoms of power, arrogance, selfishness, egocentricity, vanity, exclusivity, and self-justification, is the major cause of our sickness, misery, and unhappiness today, not only physically and mentally but also socially and ideologically.

Swimming in these waters, human beings are no longer here to find their greater purpose in life, an unfolding of the soul. Instead, they are here to seek out knowledge and to be free—free to live out their desires, fulfill their dreams and egoistic ambitions, amaze their senses, and be consumed by greed, violence, and illusion.

Humans are here to satisfy the body and the ego. They are here to ride the Dark Horse.

PART I

MAN SEPARATES FROM HEAVEN

Basically, modern man has become unhealthy because he is acting unnaturally, and he is acting unnaturally because he has separated from heaven, from nature, and from his Self.

—*Lama Nicholas*

CHAPTER 1

THE OTHER WORLD

*I*f we want to understand the mentality of our age as it is being fueled by duality, materialism, science, and the secular world—and understand the principal reason why individuals are thinking, acting, and feeling the way they are as social and material beings and not as spiritual ones—then we must go way back in time to the Greeks, specifically to Plato and Aristotle, and look at how they came to influence humanity and its interpretation of reality first by separating humanity from heaven.

Plato and Aristotle very much make up the history and evolution of Western philosophy, Western religion, Western science, Western art, Western politics, Western ethics, Western values, and Western beliefs. In a word, they have had a hand in almost all the belief systems most people share today, and their ideas influence the way we run our lives at group and individual levels.

Also, it is with these two great thinkers that we can first come to understand Westerners and their worldview and how they started to articulate reality in dualistic and antagonistic terms—terms that would eventually define how most people on this planet think and act today. At the same time, by briefly examining both Plato and Aristotle, we can also come to understand why Westerners started to remove themselves from nature and to plant the seeds of artificiality that we see so much today.

Basically, Plato saw two worlds—this world and the other world—and he established a sharp and opposing division between the two. There is the visible world—this world—and there is the other world—the invisible world. In the visible, manifest world, there is belief and distinction, earth, body, illusion, and artificiality. In the invisible world, there is the ideal/heaven, the good/God, the eternal, and the real.

So with Plato we see how reality was viewed in terms of ideals, which were outside of the body and in another world. Reality could not be known here on Earth, in our bodies; instead, it could only be known above and beyond Earth and outside of us.

According to him, our senses cannot interpret such ideals as they are locked into the mundane world of the body; they can only give us illusions. But the soul can see reality since it belongs to the other world. So the only way of interpreting this otherworldly reality is with an otherworldly entity: the soul.

Thus, this world reality is not real for Plato, at least not as we consider it here on Earth; only the other world is real. If we want to know reality and the real world, we must return to the other world; it cannot be known in this world, which is a world of illusion.

Nature, for Plato, is not the nature of this earth—the one we can perceive with our senses—but a supreme and absolute reality that transcends time and space. It is transcendent, i.e., it is out there in heaven, and the ruler is the good/God. And again, one can only apprehend this realm with the soul—not with the body and its senses—by transcending this world of illusion.

To be sure, there are images in this world, and humans perceive these images with their senses. But those who see the images see only shadows of reality, and those who make principles, values, and distinctions of these images are making only man-made or artificial distinctions, not actual ones. The only way to see the real world is not with our eyes but with the soul; only its "eye" can see the nature of reality.

But according to Plato, humans are unable to see the underlying nature of reality—the good/God and the ideal/heaven—because they rely on their senses to interpret nature (reality), and as such, humans get an unreliable and inaccurate picture of the real reality, which is not here but out there. The truth is not reflected by our senses or by the things we can feel and touch, or "on the wall in a dark cave." Rather, the truth is outside—and out there—in the light.

As Plato perceived reality, everything, without exception, in this world of ours is impermanent—including our senses and ourselves—and as a result cannot be real. Only that which is permanent and eternal can be real. Everything else is but an imitation or duplicate of something else— something whose ideal (real) form has a permanent and indestructible existence, but which is outside of space and time, and therefore, outside of our bodies and outside of any sensory perception.

Thus, there can be no such thing as reliable knowledge of this world that is presented to our senses because everything without exception is forever changing and impermanent. Hence everything is unreal, illusory, and deceptive. Paradoxically, although everything is forever changing and impermanent, the world—indeed, the whole universe—seems to exemplify order. There is change to be sure, and that is a constant, but it is a change with structure and with patterns based on harmony and proportion. This you can see in the shapes and forms of geometry and the universal numbers.

This order is not perceptible to our senses; it is invisible. It is real, it exists, and it is what constitutes the underlying reality of everything on Earth and elsewhere. It is what organizes—indeed, it is the organizing principle—and without it there can be no life. It is spirit, and without spirit, there can be no order and no vitality; hence, there can be no life.

This view of Plato's resulted in reality being divided into two realms: there is this world (the visible realm or the world of matter), an impermanent world, where nothing lasts and nothing stays the same. It's a world in which we see with our senses, but what we see is in a state of constant change and transformation—thus, a world of illusion.

Then there is the other world -an outer world, a timeless and unchanging world, and a transcendent and spiritual reality in which nothing is changing. It is a world of which humans only get a brief and fleeting glimpse, if at all, and which is accessible only to the soul. This timeless world represents the real world and the real reality because it alone is changeless, stable, and permanent.

This would be the world of heaven, the ideal, and the good/God of which we are a part because we have souls that belong to and begin there before they descend to this earth. This world is real, and only through the soul can we become aware of it.

These two realms can also be seen in humans. The first one is seen in our bodies and in the world of our senses. Like everything else on the earth, these physical bodies of ours come into existence and pass away. They are always impermanent, imperfect, and never the same—not even for a moment. They will eventually deteriorate and die like every other perishable item. The body is the mortal part of humanity.

The other part is the soul, the immortal part, which gives humans a gateway to something beyond this world of matter and impermanence. The soul lets us look into a world that is timeless, nonmaterial, and indestructible—the world of God. And like God's world, the soul is permanent and indestructible.

This soul, according to Plato, is our permanent form, different from our body, and beyond the dimensional world of physics. Its true residence belongs in a timeless, spaceless reality—not in this world but in the outer world. On Earth it is a prisoner of the body and all its delusions, but it belongs to the outer world, to the only real reality. It belongs to heaven.

This view of reality in transcendental terms later became the worldview of Christians (though they changed the good to God and the other world to heaven). It represents a time in the history of the West when individuals began to think that they must leave their bodies to apprehend truth.

It also represents a time when individuals came to believe that humans are not real—indeed, that nothing is real—and that they do not belong here. They believed that the individual is a soul that belongs elsewhere, in another world, but which is sadly imprisoned here, in this body, on this earth.

CHAPTER 2

THIS WORLD

*A*long comes Aristotle, Plato's best student, who declares that humans are no abstraction; they are real and the stuff of this world. Individuals are material beings—not ethereal ones—and the ideal cannot be created or discovered independent of the actual, which is our body here on Earth.

For Aristotle, there is only one world that we can do any thinking about, and that is the world we live in and experience. It is this world—the real world—and not another world. Whatever is outside all possibility of experience for us can be nothing for us. We have no effective way of referring to it or talking about it; therefore, it cannot enter into our philosophical reflections in any reliable way.

Reality can only be interpreted with the body and what it experiences in this world. If we want to intelligently understand the world, we should always understand that it is *this* world that we are trying to make sense of and experience personally, as well as within this body.

Aristotle cautioned people to take into account their own experiences—the experiences that actually present themselves to them—now and here on Earth. He advised them to keep referring back to their experiences at every stage because it is in investigating and understanding these experiences that we find humanity's reason for being here in the first place.

(It is for this reason that the Church initially found his words so threatening and as a consequence burned all his books and suppressed his works for centuries. One could not question the scriptures; they were sacred truths. To test them to be true or not would be sacrilege.)

So with Aristotle the gloves come off, and the division comes out in plain view. This body of mine is the source of nature, and the only source of reality that we can know is within nature—in this body and on this earth—which belongs to this world and not another world. Reality is not transcendental; it is experiential.

In other words, ideas in the intellect can never be known if the body cannot experience them. If they cannot be known, how can they be real and absolute? They have to be experienced to be real, to be known, and they can only be experienced in the body and by the body.

What Plato called the "ideas,'" Aristotle called the "essences." For Plato, soul is the essence of the body but prior to body. For Aristotle, the essences of things, though indestructible like the soul, are nevertheless the essences of *things*. So, he argued, these essences cannot remain on hold in heaven without connection to this world and to the body of perception. So when the body dies, the soul must part with it.

For Aristotle an idea cannot be an abstraction, nor can it be transcendental and reside in another realm. For it to be an idea at all, we must have knowledge of its essence. If the essence of the good is not good, neither is the essence of reality real, nor the essence of unity, one.

Thinking that we could know reality without "knowing" it—without experiencing it personally and directly—was ludicrous; it was like taking our dreams to be true. For Aristotle, this was impossible because such a state is beyond our human knowledge.

Plato had to wake up. Only then would he realize that reality could only be known in this body and in this world while he is here on this planet, alive and awake.

CHAPTER 3

MAN'S PURPOSE

*A*ristotle, in resisting Plato's version of reality and arguing that we should keep our feet firmly planted on the ground, was not rejecting, however, the concept that we are nonmaterialist entities. He always saw the true essence of any object, including a human, as consisting not only of the matter of which it is made, but also of the form, the function it performs, and its immaterial cause for being.

According to Aristotle, nothing is what it seems to be. A thing is a thing by virtue of its form, not only its material components. But if we want to understand the true nature of something—its form—we must first ask what a thing does. Only then we can understand what it is. In other words, we must first know its purpose

For example, a house must be made of something like wood and nails. But wood and nails alone do not constitute a house; the house must come together in a particular shape or form that distinguishes it as a house. To be a house it must have a purpose, such as a place for people to sleep together as a unit, which distinguishes it from, for example, a place where people sleep only for a night like a hotel.

In other words, for a building to qualify as a house, everything needs to be put together in a certain way, with a specific and detailed structure and a specific purpose. It is by virtue of that structure and purpose a house. To be sure, a house has to be made of some material, but it is not the materials that make the house; it has to have structure, form, and purpose all coming together. It cannot only have a material structure and form and not a purpose.

(Aristotle would never be able to accept today's arguments propagated by many that humans only consist of their material, biochemical, and DNA components, with no inherent purpose for existing. Instead, he would look beyond the material and look for humans' "real" form.)

For him, the key point was in asking what a thing does and what it is for. But in order to find that, one would first have to find out what the purpose of that form is; in other words, what is it in the process of becoming, or what is its final cause? Thus, by understanding what a thing does, we can understand what a thing is for or what its purpose is.

Understanding the nature of humanity is no exception. Humans are not only the stuff of the earth, an elemental, atomic, molecular structure or a genetic code. Nor are they just the structure of a man or woman. They have an essence too—a soul—and that gives them their purpose, their reason for being.

The soul, according to Aristotle, is a real substance, which expresses an idea. Such a substance is the manifestation of the inner meaning and purpose of a body here on Earth. The body is not only a material substance, but it also encases the soul, which is the cause of the body's existence in the first place and the cause behind the human form.

As he saw it, the soul not only gives purpose and meaning to human life, but it is also a cause of all the other causes. It is the cause from which movement arises; it is the final cause, to which the movement is directed, in that it is here to realize itself; and it is the material cause of animate bodies. It is the real stuff of humanity.

Thus, according to Aristotle, the soul is the reason for human existence. But what is its purpose in coming here?

The world is in flux, but it is not a purposeless flux; it is an ordered flux. Nature exists because there is movement, and all things move with a purpose. Else there would be total chaos. How else could there be order without purpose?

Each thing has its own end in sight and strives to realize that end. That's what gives order. That is a thing's purpose: to move toward the direction of realizing a final goal or end. Humans are no exception, either; they are here to realize their purpose too, which is the realization of his soul.

Thus, the soul is the ideal—the formal as well as the final cause. That is the reason the soul is here, and its purpose is the realization of the essence of the soul. It produces movement because it is directed. And because it is directed, it moves everything else.

So Aristotle argues that if one desires the good/God, he or she will desire obtaining the good/God. The fact that we are aware of the idea of good/God means that we are of the good, and our purpose is to realize that goodness—not as an idea but as a fact through our own creation, which our life is. That is our purpose.

The good for Aristotle becomes the reason, and the reason forms the purpose and the point of departure, much like works of art, which an artist creates in order to see his creation.

In this way, the good is not an abstract ideal—an abstraction, as Plato maintains. Instead it is a fact that manifests as reality in the (good) way we live and express our lives, and in the way we have united the good/God with our souls and become one and the same.

Seen in this way, our reason for being here is to unify our form (our soul) with its cause for being here, which is to be one with the eternal good/God. The good/God is our essence (our soul), and how we express it here on Earth is our purpose.

Thus, the unfolding of our soul is the reason we are here, and realizing the good—the divine nature of the soul—is our purpose in life.

Plato put the forms into heaven, thus separating the real from the ideal. By bringing them back to Earth, Aristotle made the ideal real and not only something to be realized here on Earth but also our very reason for being here in the first place—our very purpose: to realize the good, the ideal/God, here on this earth and in this world.

So for Aristotle, God (the good) is the manifestation of the inner meaning of our existence and the expression of the idea. Thus, the human's purpose in life is realizing God through the good. In this way, God is not an object but a direction. That direction, which only can be known because we have a soul, is toward the best and highest that we can conceive.

Thus everything in the world is linked to God through and through. In addition, everything in the world is tied up with the soul; they go hand in glove. God is life, the essence of life, or the essence of life is God, and our purpose is to be one with God—one in the creative principle or source of all, one with everything, one with everybody, and one with life.

In this way, Aristotle sees God as the whole and the rest of the world as the parts of this God. But the parts cannot separate from the whole; likewise, the soul cannot separate from God. The same distinctions that are found in nature as a whole also must be found in humans, as these distinctions are characteristic of man's soul, too.

Aristotle likens the soul to light. Light creates actual color out of potential color. Likewise, the soul creates body out of potential body, and that is our reason for being here.

How one lives life, i.e., how one brings light to the body, is the purpose of our existence.

CHAPTER 4

THE FALL OF MAN

*A*ccording to Aristotle, we are here on Earth because our souls created us, and it is our purpose in life to unite with our creator, which we only can do by manifesting the inherent goodness/divinity of the soul. Basically we are here because the soul wants to see itself in material form like an artist wants to see his creation by putting it on canvas.

Plato does not see things so artistically. For him, we are here because our souls willed it, in the sense that our souls were unable to get control over their desires and appetites and so chose to come down here to Earth. They came not to fulfill some noble and artistic purpose, as Aristotle maintains, but because this is the most suitable place for satisfying the material desires and illusions of the dark side of our soul.

Earth is the place of material illusion, and we have come here because the pull to realize our desires and appetites for pleasure are greater than the pull to go upward to realize our spiritual desire for eternal truth and harmony.

For this reason, according to Plato, humans fall because the power of the dark side of the soul is too great, and the reasoning and spiritual parts of the soul are too weak, unable to regulate the appetites of the dark side.

When this pure, divine, and immortal entity (the soul) falls from the other world (heaven) and enters the human body—the repository of delusion and desire—it is forced to operate through matter. As a consequence, it takes on the desires and appetites of the body, which are mortal ones.

Thus, the soul becomes a prisoner here on Earth, trapped inside the body and the material world of illusion, and it is consequently forced to operate outside of its real nature and its real environment.

The soul, according to Plato, is composed of the trinity of reason, passion/pleasure, and spirit. Together they constitute a soul. Pleasure and passion symbolize the negative side of the soul, and spirit symbolizes the positive side. The negative side is attracted to the material world (of illusion), which can be gratified on Earth, and the positive side is attracted to the spiritual world (of the real), which can be realized in heaven.

If we have any hopes of returning to heaven—to the other world, the real world—we must first weaken the powers of the dark side of the soul and strengthen the spiritual and reasoning parts of the soul. But that is not an easy task since our soul is now under the influence of the body and the mortal desires of the material world. As a result, it has come to forget who it is, what it is, and where it came from.

Plato refers to these appetites and desires and the fall of man in this allegory of the chariot, which for him is a symbol of the soul's fall from heaven and the path it can take to return home and become God-like again. In this allegory, the chariot is pulled by two winged horses; one is mortal, and the other is immortal. The mortal one is dark, and the immortal one is white.

The dark one, or the Dark Horse, is passionate, indulgent, powerful, arrogant, unwilling to follow commands, and able to turn to evil since its desires are so all-consuming. It is only interested in satisfying its desires and is always pulling the chariot down to Earth, where those desires can be filled in the material world.

The white one, or the White Horse, is the spirit. It is gentle, quiet, and respectful, and it always wants to be part of nature, where it can find peace, stillness, and serenity. It represents mystery, unity, and wholeness. Thus it pulls the chariot upward, where it can return to the source and be whole again. Driving the chariot is the charioteer. His goal is to realize the true essences of things, such as wisdom, love, courage, justice, and righteousness, and to direct the chariot back to heaven. But he cannot do this on his own; he needs assistance from the two horses, and it is his task to navigate the two horses to that end.

The charioteer must know how to tap into the strengths and minimize the weaknesses of the two horses as he guides and directs them upward to heaven. In other words, if the soul ever hopes to go home, the trinity of these three forces, which together constitute the soul, must come together in balance and unity.

But the Dark Horse is not happy going upward; on the contrary, it wants to go downward to the world below to satisfy its dark desires and passions, so it keeps pulling the chariot in the opposite direction.

If the Dark Horse is stronger than the White Horse, and the charioteer is not strong enough or determined enough to rein it in and control it, it will pull the chariot down to earth, where it must stay until the horses can grow back their wings. The regrowth of wings is quickened, or protracted, depending on the soul's experiences here on Earth. For example, if the soul is around spiritually evolved people, and if it experiences positive episodes and natural environments that give it a glimpse into the Other World, these experiences will help it to understand its divine origins; this knowledge will facilitate a faster return. But if the soul surrounds itself with artificiality, evil people, and all-consuming desires, it could be a long, long time before it can soar back to the heavens.

The longer the soul stays on Earth, the greater the risk that it will eventually forget from where it came and why it is here. Instead it will come to think that this reality on Earth—in this body, with all its delusions— is the ultimate form and representation of reality. It will thus make no attempt to improve itself and never come to perceive another reality.

Though it may yearn to separate itself again and gain release from the body and go home, that is not so simple anymore. The soul, by virtue of appropriating the corporeal world of the body and its desires here on Earth, becomes accustomed to the world of things and comes to take them as real and desirable.

At the same time, while imprisoned in the body, the soul becomes frightened of the immaterial and invisible world—even ignorant of it. Instead it becomes engrossed in the world of matter and illusion since, like art, it gives the appearance of reality, permanence, and certainty.

The soul, which now becomes attached to desire, no longer wants to go back to "the fatherland" and begins to look for another outlet, another body, and another life after death—a rebirth, where the Dark Horse can continue to express and realize the cravings and unfulfilled desires it experienced in this lifetime.

For Plato, the ultimate goal in life is to try to transcend human desire and become an ideal human—a mirror of the divine on Earth, in form and manner. To do this, however, humans have to get control over their senses and not become slaves to them. And in order to do this, they have to get control of the Dark Horse, the body of desire that keeps them attached to their senses, their passions, and the world of desire and illusion.

This does not mean renouncing desire, or the Dark Horse per se, but rather subordinating the desires of the Dark Horse under the control of reason, which is not only the lord of the body but also the lord of the soul.

According to Plato, we all existed before, and it is our job to remember that preexistence. In other words, we have gotten off the track by forgetting who and what we really are, and we can only get back on track by remembering who we were and where we came from.

The key is for the soul to have experiences that help it to remember what it truly is and where it came from. This kind of truth is not a process of learning as it is commonly considered nowadays, but of remembering what we once knew, who we really are, and where we came from—and it can only be found within.

But we will never remember who we once were, why we are here, and where we came from until we can get control of the Dark Horse and stop letting it pull our soul toward duality and artificiality and in the direction of deception and evil—into the world of smoke and mirrors and the world of illusion.

CHAPTER 5

THE WORLD OF ILLUSION AND ART

*I*n Aristotle, we have one who defends art, since he sees God as the main source of creativity and the soul as God's natural artistic expression here on Earth. For Aristotle, the soul is synonymous with God, the creative, with art itself. It is humanity's essence and purpose, and the [artistic] signature it puts on its creation—its life—is the reason for being.

In Plato, we have one who attacks art and sees art as one of humanity's greatest deceptions. It should be avoided at all costs because it excites and stimulates the senses and the mind, and as a result, it attracts people to the world of illusion.

He would vehemently oppose Aristotle's vision of reality because he would see the human soul as naturally divided between a positive force and negative one, and he would see art as the primary way of keeping humanity forever leaning to the negative side of the soul and a slave to its desires and illusions.

For Plato, this world is not real; it is an illusion, and we are hopelessly lost—imprisoned in an alien body and a slave to the Dark Horse and its delusions. Our purpose is to save, or liberate, our souls. This we can only do by getting control over the Dark Horse and uplifting the spiritual side of our souls, the White Horse, to get our souls to return to the real world—the world of the good/God and the ideal/heaven—where we really belong.

In the art world, however, everything is man-made and artificial; it is a world of sense and sensibility, not spirituality. It is an unreal projection constructed by humans, not in the least bit representative of the real world out there. If we rely on our senses to perceive this reality, as we do with art, we will only get illusory representations. So how will we ever know what is true and real and be motivated to return home?

The objects of our senses, according to Plato, are no more real than a painter's representation of reality, so dwelling on what we perceive with our senses is like dwelling on the images of a painting, a movie, or a computer screen and taking them to be real.

But the world of art does exactly that; it attracts us to the images and shadows and convinces us that they are real; therefore, we want to possess them. In this way, art misrepresents reality in the sense that it gets us to think the artificial world is real, and the natural and mysterious world is unreal.

Thus, if we want to know the real truth, and if we want to guide the soul safely to liberation, first we must steer clear of the world of illusion. But how can we do that if we are under the influence of the world of art?

If we hope to gain control of the Dark Horse, we have to first remove our self from illusion. But in order to do that, we have to distance the soul from the objects of the senses and the body's desires, which only create attachments and subsequently delude the mind and lead it to become a servant of the body.

Art and man-made projections of reality represent one of the greatest risks to our souls, as well as one of the greatest impediments to our quest for truth and self-realization. Not only are they keeping us addicted to our senses, but they are also keeping us more attracted to the illusory world, as opposed to renouncing it.

For this reason, Plato was strongly opposed to art and the artificial world. First, he saw the art world as being only representational, not factual or real, and as such, illusory. Second, it had such a powerful appeal to the senses, the very things that keep humans bound to this phenomenal world and the world of illusion.

If we want to free the soul, we must take care of our true nature, which is our God nature, and not cater to the needs of our body nature and the world of illusion. In other words, we must steer clear of art. By focusing on the world of art and artificiality—not the world of the soul—we plant the seeds of duality, and in the process, we separate our soul from the source.

Plato believed that the goal of life is to acquire a grasp of the world of ideals in which the soul exists and to continue to exist for all of eternity. In order to do that, we must be able to pierce the surface of the ephemeral that constitutes the world of the senses and penetrates to the level of underlying reality. If we want to experience an ideal, we can only experience it to be real without the senses.

For example, if we are to understand the underlying reality of an ideal like love, we must first free our self of our senses and their attractions, i.e., we must first free our self of the physical/sexual part. In this way we will experience the ideal love, not the artificial love.

For Plato, the only real harm that can come to a person is when he or she harms the soul. But that is exactly what art does; it attracts us to the world of senses, fuels the desires of the Dark Horse, and holds us back from our true calling—that is, to soar above the level of our senses and the material world to the timeless and non-sensory realm beyond, and to the ideal world, or the real world of the soul and God.

This other world, where we can gather a true idea of good/God, is not here but out there, and it is only there that we can find out what we really are but not in an artificial world.

CHAPTER 6

THE BIG SPLIT

*P*lato and Aristotle agreed that we are inherently divine in nature; we are the stuff of our souls, and we are here because of our souls. But it was the way in which they interpreted the nature of the soul and how it came to earth—and how it manifests—that brought out so many differences and distinctions.

And it was also the way in which they interpreted the soul and humanity's purpose and why it came to Earth—whether humans are inherently good and their purpose in life is to bring out this (divine) goodness, or inherently bad and their purpose in life is to extricate themselves from evil, this body, and this world of illusion.

On the one hand, we see Westerners' perception of reality as influenced by Platonic thought, in which the real world is not here but in another world. Accordingly, God and nature are not here among us, but in another world and another realm. Since we reside in a relative, materialistic, and impermanent world, we are unable to perceive the true nature of God or reality.

With Plato, God is the only reality but a reality that cannot be seen or perceived in this world. God exists but in another place, imperceptible to humans on Earth. We are not here to unfold our souls but to save them, especially from the passions and delusions of the Dark Horse.

Since we are living in this world, we cannot apprehend the ideal world of the good/God because we are hostages to this mortal body and can only perceive relative perspectives of reality as projected by the senses. We are very much outside of God—and the good—because we are controlled by the desires of the Dark Horse and, as a consequence, live in the world of illusion.

Plato represents a type of thought that runs through the course of Western history and which has influenced the way Westerners perceive reality, even up to today. With him we get the first real division in Western humanity—a sense of duality in which humans see themselves as being divided between this and another world, as being of this earth and not of this earth, as being immortal and mortal, and as being good and bad.

This division would take root in Westerners with the dichotomy between the soul and the body. Over time, the soul would no longer be divided into three parts as Plato defined it, with the Dark Horse running roughshod over the spiritual side of the human soul, or the White Horse. Instead, Westerners would come to see the soul as wholly pure and divine, ready to fly off to heaven but held back by the body.

Thus, the body and its senses would come to define humans' unhealthy and unholy nature, not the dark side of their soul. A clear duality would begin to emerge in Western thinking between what is pure and right and what is impure and wrong. The pure would come to represent the divine and the immaterial world, and the impure would come to represent the mundane and the material world.

On the other hand, we see a reality that is influenced by Aristotelian thought, in which the real can only be experienced here in this world; God is not somewhere outside of humanity but within us all. We are one with Him by experiencing Him through love. Thus, God is love, and by our souls abiding in love, God abides in humankind. It is in the unfolding of the soul that we realize that.

With Aristotle, we see that God is not a being which exists in a reality; God *is* reality, and we exist within God. God isn't in any particular place; God is the place, and every place we live in is God. God is one, the innermost self of all, so we are all of one form. It is important to unite with Him here, not try to go somewhere else to find Him.

Aristotle brings everything down to Earth, including God and the good, so in this way reality comes to be defined by how we experience it in the world, through our bodies, in the phenomenal world. Thus, nothing beyond our understanding and beyond our knowledge can be real; it has to be proved to be real.

Westerners would not only be pulled in opposite directions by Plato's and Aristotle's metaphysical perspectives, but they would also be pulled in opposing directions by their perspectives in politics: one drawing them in the direction of realizing the greater good for communal ideals (Plato), and the other (Aristotle) leading them in the greater good for individual ideals and happiness.

So in effect what we see through these two great thinkers is the genesis of the big split in the Western world between the visible and the invisible, the material and the immaterial, heaven and Earth, the real and the unreal, the soul and the body, the intellect and the mind, the individual and the community, and later, between religion and science.

Basically, we are getting two alternatives, two horses to ride, but only given one choice to make—and we come to be split in two.

CHAPTER 7

THE FIRSTBORN

*P*lato and Aristotle, as well as some of the early Greek philosophers, represent the emergence of rational thinking in the West. They were trying to understand the world by use of their reason, without appealing to superstition, religion, faith, revelation, tradition, or authority. They were also teaching other people to use their reason, too, and to think for themselves, so they did not expect others, not even their own students, to agree with them.

The relationship between Plato and Aristotle best illustrates that even though they differed in their views, they both were following the philosophy of Socrates, who taught that people's first priority in life is to their personal integrity in terms of duty to themselves, and not to the gods, not to the laws, not the authorities, and not to their teacher.

These two conflicting philosophies between Plato and Aristotle, as well as their approaches to truth and reality, have characterized Western philosophy and culture from practically the beginning of Western civilization. Initially they were articulated as Platonic and Aristotelian philosophy, but later these conflicting thoughts would find expression in the opposing views of religion and science, and democracy and authoritarianism.

Those who have subscribed to Plato's worldview have set a primary value on God and heaven and have given a secondary value to knowledge of the world as it presents itself to our senses. They have shunned the body and stressed the soul.

And those who have set a primary value on knowledge of this world have accepted Aristotle's worldview, stressing the material world and the world as experienced with the senses. They have shunned the soul and given importance to the intellect.

Christianity would be the first born out of this dualistic way of perceiving reality, and it would take Plato's transcendental way of seeing truth and reality and plant it in the fertile minds of post-Roman Westerners.

Like Plato, the early Christians maintained that our primary concerns need to be with examining something that lies beyond this world. They also believed, like Plato, that humanity's ultimate purpose in life (Aristotle's final cause) is to transcend this impermanent world of suffering and go beyond to the heavenly world or the realm of ideals. So in picking up where Plato left off, the early Christians supported his claim that ultimate reality consists of ideal forms in another world. But they elaborated on his version, arguing that these ideals must be mental. This was markedly different from Aristotelian thought, which looked at the human body and how humans experience it as the beginning and end of reality.

In advancing that ideals are mental, the early Christians argued that mind is the ultimate reality since it precedes matter, not the body. Though the body may apprehend reality through the senses, it is relative reality because the body is only a receptacle and not the original cause. Actual reality precedes form; indeed, it comes from formlessness. In other words, they established that mind—not material stuff or the form of essences—creates matter. If humans only rely on their bodies and their experiences to understand reality, they will get a distorted picture of truth because nothing begins with a material causation; it begins with a mental one. Thought is necessary for something to be created, and humans should look to consciousness, not the body or the matter, to know the creator and the original cause.

So the first principle of their newborn dogma would be that mind—not the body and intellect as Aristotle argued—is the source of all creation, deriving first from the mind and consciousness of God.

Secondly, in looking at Plato's good/God, the early Christians put forward a belief that there are three ascending levels of being. The first level is the lowest, the level of the soul. Human beings are on this level. The middle level is the intellect, on which the ideal forms are understood. And the highest level is the good, where contemplative and meditative human beings are engaged and endeavor toward oneness with the good/God. This would become the second principle of Christian dogma: Humankind cannot come to know truth intellectually, only intuitively.

As for the soul, it would become transcendent and immortal—a clear and separate entity outside of the body, which belongs in the City of God. It would not be an independent soul anymore, as Plato maintained, nor would it be driven by the desires of the Dark Horse and White Horse, each one balancing the other. Instead it would become a soul that God has condemned to Earth because of its sinful ways.

In this way, the Church would look at the soul as an entity that is here, not because it had chosen to come here because the Dark Horse wanted to realize its desires like an artist, as Aristotle had claimed, but because God condemned it here.

Thus, humans are no longer responsible for being here, nor are they free to go home; they are prisoners on Earth. Whether they go to heaven or not depends on the goodwill and grace of God; otherwise, they will be sent to hell.

So we see that the two worlds—the visible and the invisible, and the ideal and the good that Plato spoke of—are evident in Christianity, and the purpose of humanity, as decreed first by Plato, is to rise up and be one with God.

The Church appropriated Plato's dualistic arguments in the main with one exceptional difference. With Plato, humans were free to leave the Dark Horse and ascend to heaven on their own, which they could only do with the help of the White Horse, the spiritual part in the soul. But with the Church, humans lose this freedom—and they later lose the White Horse and the spiritual part, too.

Instead, human beings are now beholden to God's grace and the Church's grace to allow them to return to heaven. By the same token, humans can no longer get to know God directly; they have to go through a vicar of Christ to know God, and personal experience is disallowed.

Now the stage is set for constructing the edifice of duality in the West, The first cornerstone, on which the foundation is erected, starts with Christianity and its perception of reality as mirrored in Plato's two main philosophical teachings: that the world has been created in the mind of God, and human beings are aspiring to oneness with God, who is perfect goodness and love.

Establishing how the world was created, and by whom, and coming up with rationally contrived explanations of humanity's purpose in life, and how to realize it, were inadequate methods for discovering God and purpose because, as they saw it, real knowledge transcends both the senses and the intellect.

Like the body, the self is not real; it is impermanent and undergoing changes just like everything else in the phenomenal world. So how can one use the intellect, which is a part of the body and hence ephemeral, to define truth, which is all pervading, never changing, and permanent? One can never arrive at truth by following the intellect and the rigors of logic; truth can only be derived at a sublime level. So instead of begging their followers to ask questions and seek their own answers as in the Greek tradition—and coming up with rationally based conclusions to justify their beliefs—the early Christians initially departed in large part from the intellectual requirements of Greek thinking and asked their followers instead to have faith and "to believe because it is absurd."

Naturally, with the ascension of this newly emerging, faith-based paradigm, the supporters of rational and critical thinking would suffer tremendously. After all, if the self is not real, then the product of the self's reasoning powers could not be real and valid, either. So they, along with the teachings of Aristotle, were not only disparaged and discouraged, but they also were summarily forbidden and banned respectively.

This way of thinking—or nonthinking—would become the first pillar of duality in the West.

CHAPTER 8

THE GREAT CULTURAL REVOLUTION IN THE WEST

In the last days of the Roman Empire, the Western world was scattered and confused. People valued what they had learned on their own, thus questioning what the ancient philosophers had established.

Individuality reigned supreme, and as a result, there was great diversity and no sense of unity, only disarray. Law, instructions, and any form of authority were ignored and largely discredited. Thus, it was no accident that under these conditions the imperial power of Rome declined and eventually fell.

It is also not surprising that when the Church arrived on the scene in Rome, it first wanted to establish control. It chose to do so by severing Westerners' memory of the ancient past and installing a whole new way of thinking on pure and empty minds, void of previous conditioning.

Thus, under the Vatican, all Roman historical records, save those kept in custody by the Church, were burned. In the new "state" of the Church, the ruler would be the pope, and there would be no literature, books, or records by the Romans or Greeks; only the laws of the Church and the teachings of the scriptures as written in the Bible were allowed.

The purpose was obvious. The Church wanted unity among the people, not diversity, and the only way that could be affected was by having a unification of thought. So it would have to ensure there would be but one world, one government, one history, and one way of thought.

In this new world of unity, there would be no works by former rulers or philosophers, only the official acts of the Vatican. Thus, anything not in the Bible or the teachings of the Church would be curtailed and not allowed to progress further.

Individuals who might want to study could only take their teachings from priests. Henceforth, no diversity of thought and opinion would be permitted, and people could not have diverse doctrines or beliefs, either. Historical philosophies, especially Aristotle's, with their varying schools, positions, and ideas, would be burned and banned. Thus began the Great Cultural Revolution in the West and the revolution of Christianity. Any memory of Rome—its history, teachings, gods and goddesses, rites and rituals, traditions and customs—would be erased from Westerners' memory. And the Greeks and their contribution to Western civilization and culture would also be wiped out. For the next one thousand years, Westerners would only know one truth, one reality, and one way of thinking: the Bible, the scriptures, and the history of Jesus and how the Church interpreted them.

All this would be enforced under a feudalistic society in which there was no separation of religion, education, economy, and politics. So for more than a thousand years, Westerners would be the victims of a cultural revolution—a revolution so vast, so deep, and so complete that it belies belief.

It is truly unfathomable, the extents to which Westerners were stripped of their past, their ancestry, and their cultural heritage. Everything had been taken from them, even their collective memory—and for as long as a thousand years!

For all intents and purposes, Westerners had lost any sense of freedom, as they were only permitted to see one reality and as such, could only live a life in accord with that reality. They had no other choices. The other choices, the ones of their own diverse cultural heritage and the ones advanced by the ancient Greek and European cultures, had been taken away. Now there was only one choice, and that was the one brought in from the Church of Rome.

Over time, the Church slowly and systematically denuded the West of its culture, so much so that it was no longer in a position to understand and relate to its cultural heritage or what it meant to its people. For all intents and purposes, humanity had become a Christian, and in the process, it was robbed of its past and the link that connected people to their past. The West's cultural heritage and philosophical interpretations of truth and reality were completely ripped from its consciousness.

With its regulations in place, the Church would go on to rule over Westerners for many centuries to come, and it was able to do so because it had the power to rule over them. Now the Church would rule over humanity, both in terms of its body and its mind—the secular world and the world of spirit. The ways of the Church and Western culture would become one and the same.

To get an idea of just how comprehensive the Cultural Revolution in Europe was, compare it to China under Mao Tse-tung and that cultural revolution. Like the Church, Mao—who was also bringing in a foreign philosophy—tried wiping out traditional Chinese culture, which he did by burning all the books, destroying all the traditional buildings and temples, and imprisoning or killing all the teachers of the former culture.

He then went on to "educate" the people, which he did by controlling what, where, and by whom they learned. Mao wanted to start with the young people, so he wiped the board clean by emptying their little minds of any "corrupting" influence, such as traditional Chinese culture, and by de-constructing older people from their former beliefs.

Nobody was allowed to read anything but Mao's *Little Red Book*, and the Party strictly controlled all contents. The people were forced back into the countryside to live in communes, where they were indoctrinated on a daily basis. No individuality was permitted, and no freedoms were tolerated, and artistic expression was strictly prohibited.

The Cultural Revolution was so complete that few people today have any recollection of their ancient Chinese history and cultural heritage, apart from what the Party lets them know about it. But this cultural revolution of Mao's would eventually fail and be considered one of the great tragedies in Chinese history. And it only lasted less than half a century!

Power manifests in two ways: by having control over another's body and by having control over another's mind. To control another's body, there must be a rule of law in place and an efficient way of enforcing the rule of law. To control another's mind, there must be a strict system of education in place and an efficient way of enforcing what is taught, how it's taught, and where it's taught.

When one has control over another's body, one has control over another's movement as well. When one has control over another's mind, one has control over another's perception of truth and reality. To have *real* power, not relative power, one would control both mind and body, and simultaneously control another's freedom and perception of truth and reality.

If one has control only over another's body, the risk is always great that the intellect will know what it does not have and thus feel discontented and, when the opportunity presents itself, rebel in order to satisfy the need for personal freedom and knowledge. Tyrannical governments eventually end up this way because the rule of law and might is no match for the human quest for freedom and independence.

If one has control over another's intellect, one can condition the mind. Then the other is in no position to know what he or she does not know, or long for what he or she does not possess. Thus the individual will not rebel since there is no world of opposites, just one world of thought and activity, and he or she can have no way of comparing and feeling discontent in the mind.

Now consider the Western world under the Church. Their former cultures had not only been destroyed, but they also had been wiped out, physically and intellectually. All temples were torn down and churches erected on top of them; all their books had been burned, and their religions and philosophies had been banned; and the people were forced to live in the countryside, and they were not permitted to learn anything but the contents of the Bible.

There was a committee of cardinals, bishops, and priests who ruled over the people and their lands, and nobody had direct access to any of them. All came under one roof of the Church with only one purpose in mind: to control the people. In the process, Westerners lost their individual freedoms, and creativity was stifled.

From the end of the Roman Empire, the Church and its anti-intellectual, faith-based paradigm gripped the West. For close to a thousand years it ruled all aspects of Western life, leaving no area outside of its control.

Quite different from the Greeks' perception of reality and their way of investigating the nature of being and phenomena, which was based on humans being free to examine both, Westerners lost all of their freedoms under the Church, including the ability to express their innate quality of curiosity, investigation, and inquiry.

Now there was only one way to interpret reality and only one way to express it—and the Church regulated and defined them. By also controlling the soul, the Church made its power absolute! It controlled everything in the West, and like ignorant children, the people became hopelessly and completely dependent.

But one group dared to take exception to this Church control, and it would pay dearly for its defiance.

CHAPTER 9

THE FIRST CASUALTY

*S*pirituality would be the first casualty in the West with the arrival of Christianity and humanity's separation from heaven. Reason and intellect would be under siege with the prevailing faith-based mentality, but both would rebound in later times and ironically become instrumental in later eradicating spirituality from the West.

Catharism was a name given to a spiritual movement that started in the West around the eleventh century and flourished in the twelfth and thirteenth centuries. It represented the first real internal threat to the Church, a homegrown movement (as opposed to the Moors/Muslims from the outside) that took place in the West, one that questioned both the Church's interpretation of Jesus and its interpretation of the scriptures.

It was a movement that protested against the moral decay and corruption of the Church, which was endemic at that time, claiming it was "full of dogs and hypocrites" and against what it perceived to be a total lack of understanding of the nature of the reality. But most importantly, it was a movement that questioned the Church's spiritual authority.

The Cathars were spiritualists, thus they rejected the material world, which they believed was imprisoning the human soul. They also rejected the Church's interpretation of morality and any rules and codes of conduct as decreed by the Church, saying they were man-made, hence artificial and not real. They were even opposed to marriage, a man-made convention.

According to the Cathars, the Church had become obsessive about ritualism, indulging in the practice for its own selfish needs. It was stuck with words and phrases, guilty of reciting beautiful scriptures and hymns for the Church's own sake. For the Cathars, rituals were designed to purify the mind and prepare the devoted for the ultimate stage of realization; they were the first step for God realization.

The Church, however, had sunk into rituals as an end in itself; it had become too preoccupied with chanting hymns and eulogizing the glories of Jesus. The Church was performing the various rituals with a definite materialistic and selfish motive behind it, believing that these rituals would earn the Church the fulfillment of its mundane desires. But in the process, it had lost sight of humanity's spiritual roots and true origin.

This way of religion did not truly aspire to or attempt to reach the supreme state of God unity. It was instead obsessed with worldly desires and had become shortsighted; it was all about people observing certain rites solely for attaining pleasure and power. In this way, the Church was too far removed from God and His true nature, lost instead in ritual, power, materialism, and sensual gratification.

Their minds were too focused on the passions, affairs, and pleasures of this world; they were ruled by their senses and did not direct their intellect to the transcendental reality and the other world. For this reason, the Cathars were interested in reviving a spiritual foundation to Christianity, and they admonished the people to follow nature and its natural ways as manifested through the spirit.

The Cathars' philosophy, much like Plato's, maintained that this material world is not real, just an illusion, based on ignorance of the real. For something to be the real, it must exist at all times—in the past, in the present, and in the future; it is enduring and persists in all periods of time, thus it is eternal and unchanging. This world is not the real, and all those who inhabit a body in this world are also not real because everything is subject to change—transient, fleeting, and passing.

Naturally, seen in this light, the Cathars would have problems defining Jesus in the flesh and calling Him the Son of God. The Son of God could not, according to them, incarnate in flesh. This would make Him subject to change, impermanent and mortal, and as such, He was not a god, not the real.

For people to worship Jesus in that form is tantamount to worshipping an illusion, which is steeped in ignorance of the real, like art. Thus, the Cathars rejected the (materialistic) Trinitarian dogma of the Church, which saw Jesus of the flesh. They also rejected the Church's interpretation of the Holy Spirit as something that is outside of humanity. Instead they saw Jesus as a human form of a spirit or angel, not as the Son of God who had come down from heaven in human flesh. And they saw the Holy Spirit as residing in us all. In essence, they rejected the core of the Church, considering it materialistic, spiritless, and an unreal representation of the real.

This world, according to the Cathars, though not the real, is pervaded by the real. Most people know the real as God. Since God pervades the whole world, He naturally is embodied in humans. The way in which God pervades humans is in the form of the spirit. Like God, the spirit is all-pervading and omnipresent, and it exists in all sentient beings and inert objects. The body-mind-intellect defines the individual human personality, but beyond the material equipment of the body-mind-intellect lays the spirit. This, according to the Cathars, is the core of the human being. Every human being has this same spiritual core—the all-pervading spirit.

Human bodies may be different, and people may manifest in different ways and forms. But the spirit within them is all one. Indeed, it is the spirit functioning through the various bodies that causes the variety of human beings and gives them life and vitality. It is our mission in life to find our true spirit and to merge it with God.

But to do this we must be free to let our spirits soar and unfold naturally. We cannot have others telling us what is real or not and what is moral and not; we already know that naturally because the truth lies within. But we must be able to experience it ourselves. Naturally, this kind of thinking would not sit well with the Church authorities.

As Catharism was spreading rapidly through Europe, the Church perceived its followers as a direct threat to its power and initiated a crusade to extinguish the movement. Hundreds of thousands of people were killed. Then, to make sure there wasn't a single Cathar left on Earth, the Church launched the medieval inquisition to kill every member of the sect. This time it was successful, and the Cathars were extinguished from Europe forever—all of them!

The writing was on the wall. The greatest threat to the Church was coming from within, in the form of the spiritualists—people who lived and thrived on faith, love, devotion, and most of all, spirit. If the Church hoped to survive another onslaught, it would have to be better prepared. But it would not be able to defeat spiritualists with the sword alone. It would have to rely on something far more powerful to beat them: reason.

The panicked Church countered these trends by turning away from Plato, and his more esoteric interpretations of reality, and adopting Aristotle as its greatest defender. This way the Church suppressed any movement channeled directly from the spirit world and God, and not as interpreted by its priests and the intellect. Henceforth, it would categorically reject esoteric beliefs and rationales.

So in what may be considered one of the greatest reversals in the history of the West, as well as one of the greatest ironies {and tragedies), the Church disowned its Platonic roots and adopted Aristotelian reason and his "four causes."

(Coincidentally, this finds a parallel in modern-day Communist China, with the Falun Gong, a religious-spiritual movement. This movement, which captured the attention of a wide swath of Chinese people in a very short time span, was perceived as a direct threat to the control of the Communist Party. As a result, the party banned the religion and persecuted and imprisoned its members, numbering in tens of millions. Then, in much the same way as the Church did when it brought back the rational teachings of Aristotle to counter the growth of spirituality, the Communist Party brought back its greatest enemy, Confucius, in order to impose rationalism and restore social control.)

The very person the Church so feared the most, the very person whose books and teachings the Church had spurned—and burned—for centuries now became its liberator. Now for anything to stand up to scrutiny, it would have to pass the test of reason as articulated by Aristotle.

Henceforth arguments had to be logical and presented according to Aristotelian principles. Faith and conviction alone would not suffice, and no one could speak in tongue anymore. Thus, the Church effectively entered the intellectual world to enforce its power, and in the process, it distanced itself from the spiritual world as advocated by Plato, Plotinus, and even Jesus and the Bible. The inquisition would physically eliminate spirituality from the face of the earth in the West, and ironically, reason, intellect, and Aristotle would ensure that it was never resurrected again. The intellect—not dogma, not blind faith, not swords—would drive the last nail into the coffin of spirituality in the West, forever keeping it dead and buried.

Thus, the mind in the form of emotion and as expressed through religion would become the firstborn in the evolving dualistic Western mentality, and the intellect, in the form of reason, would become the third born. The second born, spirit, in the form of intuition and expressed through spirituality, was delivered a mortal blow in the West. Its death would come to represent the greatest casualty in the history of the West.

BURN, HERETIC, BURN

*W*hat inspires an individual and where does that inspiration come from? How can we explain the people of genius, the works of great artists, and the sudden insights and knowledge that seem to come from nowhere? What leads us to create? Is it us or something coming through us? Is it a spirit that flows through us? Do we inhale it? What is it made of? Is it in the air that we breathe? Is it in us?

What exactly is entering us, and why is it coming to us in particular? Does it flow freely through everybody, or is it always there? Do we flow through it? Does it only come from above in the form of the Holy Spirit, directed by God, as the Church maintains, or is it all around us, accessible to all? Can we access it ourselves? Are we part of it? Is it part of us? Are we souls imprisoned in a body here on this earth—as Plato and the Church maintain—separate from our Creator and heaven, yearning to return? Or are we part of it all, connected to and one with God, and as such, one with everything as Aristotle maintained?

Is God present in all of creation while still being distinct from it? Is there any place that God is not? Is everything God? And if so, are we a part of God, not separate from Him but yearning to become one with the One?

The Cathars had asked these questions and formulated their own distinct answers. But their answers and practices were considered heretical since they did not conform to Church values and beliefs, not to mention sacred scriptures. So the Cathars were eliminated. But eliminating them did not stop Westerners from asking the same questions and believing that there was something more behind our being here and something more behind our actions than simply God's will.

The Renaissance and the resurgence of humanism, philosophy, and great art in the West marks a decisive time when the West would awaken after a very long slumber and begin asking questions again. It marks a time when Westerners use their intellect again, a time when they start pursuing knowledge and abandoning dogma, and a time when they finally dare to stand up on their own two feet and take control over life here on Earth.

It represents the desire for independent inquiry and individual expression. It represents a time when humanity is greatly inspired. It represents a time when Westerners want freedom—freedom to investigate nature without any conditions and freedom to be their own person. But most importantly, it represents a time when the West is inspired to edge away from the Church and its control over society and its enforced ignorance on its people.

But it also represents a time when the concept of spirit and the spirit world comes center stage, beyond people's artistic and intellectual creations to people's expression of truth and reality, in the form of esoteric beliefs and alchemy.

Is there a secret code to everything like a "seed of life"? After all, what was actually behind all the great accomplishments of Michelangelo, da Vinci, Rembrandt, and Columbus? What was propelling them to create such works and guiding explorers to cross uncharted seas?

Is it a spirit, and if so, how can we limit it only to works of art? It must be behind everything—behind us all—in anything we create or invent. And it must also be behind our very desires, thoughts, and actions. It must be behind the mind; indeed, it must be the force behind life itself.

We cannot separate ourselves, and life, from it any more than we can separate the clouds from the atmosphere. It cannot be limited or divided, separated or isolated, and we cannot be separated or divided from it. It is the whole, and we are its part; everything we do is simply a manifestation of the unmanifest. It is part of the air we breathe, and inhaling it gives us vitality and inspiration.

The Church was willing to admit that there must be something behind the individual (it would not allow a spirit, independent of the Holy Spirit) to explain a person's incredible artistic genius. So why not call it the spirit of one's personality? That is ambiguous and harmless enough.

But to say that an individual can access something on his or her own, independent of God and the Holy Spirit, and to question the origin and creation of the universe—as well as our place in it, how and why we are here, and in what form—is quite another thing from accepting beautiful works of art. The tolerance of the Church had its limits. Besides, there was only one answer to anybody's questions, and they were all clearly stated in the words of the Bible.

One cannot access another version of truth by mystical revelation. It is impossible; it is heresy to attempt to do so, punishable by death. There is a cosmological hierarchy—with God at the top, Earth in the center, and humans running everything on God's behalf—and that is the only truth and the only reality. But times were changing in the West, and with it, the West's perception of reality was beginning to change. And with the invention of the printing press, Westerners' access to information and knowledge was expanding as well. To be sure, people were still looking up to the sky and feeling awe and wonder. But there were other types looking up there now, too, and they were beginning to see things differently.

Giordano Bruno was one such person. When Giordano Bruno looked up to the sky in the late sixteenth century, he did not see what the Church saw and consequently rejected the existing Christian cosmological view, replacing it with a heliocentric universe. In the universe he saw, all the stars were really suns like ours, around which orbited other planets like our solar system.

In this universe, our sun is nothing particular, and our place in the universe is nothing special, either. Our earth is just one more heavenly body as is our sun and God has no peculiar relation to our side of the universe any more than He has with other areas of the universe.

Bruno no longer saw a hierarchical universe; instead he saw a universe without limitation, unfathomable and infinite. In this universe, there were an infinite number of inhabited worlds like our own, with an infinite number of people like us. In other words, Bruno was seeing extraterrestrials—aliens—all over the universe!

He did not limit his theory to the heavenly bodies and extraterrestrials; God also lost His centrality in Bruno's heliocentric theory. In an infinite universe, we also get an infinite God. For Bruno, God is not above in heaven, as the Church maintained, but He is everywhere. He is an immanent God, who takes on the form of all existence, not just a far-off land called heaven. God and heaven lose their geocentric structure under Bruno.

Instead God and the universe are endless and limitless, and to that extent, infinite and indeterminable, and consequently, incomprehensible. God is as present here on Earth as He is in other places. He is immanent everywhere and accessible to all. To say that God is immanent, Bruno is saying that God is present in all of creation while still being distinct from it—like the ancient Chinese concept of the Tao.

Immortality means deathless, and it means birthless. That is the ultimate experience of Godhood, which is a state of absolute perfection. It is the real since it never ceases to be. That which is ephemeral changes and passes and cannot be the real. For God to be the real, He must be changeless, all-pervading and omnipresent.

Moreover, God also cannot be in some far-off place like heaven, regardless of how powerful He is. For God to be a god, He must be everywhere and pervade the entire world. If He is fixed in a place, such as heaven, He is separate from what is not there, so how can He be omnipresent? God is not separate from humankind somewhere out in space or in heaven. Heaven is not a geographical location that we have to go to. That was how the Church saw heaven. Going there was its ultimate destination, but it was wrong, according to Bruno.

God is everywhere, not in one fixed and separate place. Getting to heaven is symbolic of getting to a state—a transcendental place—of self-realization. It is not a specific place or a destination or a material location where you can satisfy your suprasensory desires. You do not go there; you *reach* there.

Everything is made of God, but God does nothing to create anything. He is not the creator, but nothing can exist without God. God is the essence and the spirit. All the worlds—whether they are waking or dreaming ones—arise out of God, exist in God, and ultimately merge with God.

Worlds come and go, and humans come and go, but they are all made of the stuff of God like a pot is made of clay. The human body may perish, just as the pot can break, but the clay within—the spirit—is imperishable. Nothing can cause the destruction of God. And nothing can cause the destruction of the human spirit.

Basically, what Bruno is saying is that there is no place where God is not, just as there is no place that the Tao is not. Like the Chinese Tao, God's presence extends everywhere simultaneously. The Church accused Bruno of promoting pantheism, which maintains that everything is God or is a part of God, making God part of His own creation but unable to do anything to act on His creation.

In contrast, the Church has always maintained a hierarchical and geocentric God, one who is perceived as different from and separate from His creation and in a distinct place—a God who is very much able to act on His creation. Indeed, nothing in life can exist without God first willing and creating it because everything happens in the mind of God.

Bruno, like the Cathars three hundred years before him, was tried for heresy by the Roman Inquisition on charges—in addition to promoting pantheism—of denying several core Catholic doctrines, such as the Trinity, the divinity of Christ, and the Christian notions of divine creation and the last judgment. But above all, he was tried for heresy for his mysticism.

It appears that Bruno not only was a friar, a philosopher, and a scientist, but he was also a mystic, making him especially dangerous to the Church and to his fellow colleagues in the scientific world. After all, Bruno was not a wandering troubadour, a witch speaking in tongue, or a member of the Cathar community.

Bruno was a man of the cloth—a philosopher and a scientist—who strongly believed in esotericism and strongly opposed Aristotle. This placed him squarely outside the box, neither here nor there, and that was frightening since his views were not within the purview of common discourse or refutation.

For instance, in his vision of the infinite universe, he saw it filled with an endless number of other planets like ours and an endless number of inhabitants like us, but he also saw it filled with a substance—a "pure air" or spirit or qi (chi)—that controls the perpetual becoming of all things in the universe. He saw it filled with a vital force, and this vital force is the law—and origin—of all of existence.

It is the organizing principle of nature and the force behind all life. This spirit world—or qi (chi) as the Chinese refer to it—is the bridge Plato spoke of that connects earth with heaven, matter with energy, and body with soul. This law, as he saw it, not only rejected the truth and value of the whole of Christianity but also rocked the world of materialism and science.

But how did Bruno come to know of the heliocentric solar system, which was confirmed a hundred years later by Newton (who, it must be added, also believed in ether or pure air)? Did he reach it by some mystical revelation? Was Bruno actually persecuted because he was proclaiming divine mysteries beyond the traditionally and rationally established modes of investigation, either religious or scientific? What was the real sacrilege, the real heresy that Bruno committed? Was it that he had defied Church beliefs and its cosmological hierarchy as well as the divinity of Christ and the Holy Spirit? Was it that he saw other inhabitants of heaven like us, aliens, who may have even come here in previous visitations? Was it because his conclusions were so outside Church creed and beliefs?

Or was it that he had discovered the spirit world in the West, like the world of qi (chi) in China, and the vital principle of all of life, excluded by both religion and science? Was it because he defied Aristotle and the world of purpose and the four causes? Was it because his method of investigation did not conform to scientific, rational, and materialistic standards of proof?

Whatever the real reasons, in 1600, Giordano Bruno was summoned to a room at the Vatican, where he refused to renounce his esoteric beliefs and was subsequently condemned for heresy and burned at the stake at the flower market in Rome.

As the people looked on, chanting, "Burn, heretic, burn," they had little idea that his condemnation would effectively condemn Westerners to a life of duality and materialism. For with the burning of Bruno's body, the spirit world went up in flames too, and with it the West's connection—its bridge—to heaven would be severed.

But the Western spirit did not die with the death of Bruno. As the saying goes, "Stone walls do not a prison make, nor does iron bar a cage." The walls of a prison can arrest the movement of one's body but not his thoughts. Weapons and fire can destroy the human body but not the self within. One cannot keep the spirit down forever. Eventually it must rise up.

And rise up it would—but not without further persecution. Exactly sixteen years later another person was summoned to the same room and for the same charges. His name was Galileo Galilei.

CHAPTER 11

THE GREAT LIBERATOR

For the first time in a thousand years, Westerners had started to express themselves again, to see another reality, and in the process, they started to defy the Church and its interpretation of reality. This was something nobody had been able to do for over a thousand years, not since the beginning of the great Cultural Revolution in the West.

For close to a thousand years Westerners had been told how to reach God; they were never allowed to get to Him on their own. For anything regarding religious or spiritual interpretation, one had to look to the Church for answers. Independent inquiry was not only discouraged but it also was illegal. The Cathars and Bruno had tried, and the world observed in horror where that got them.

The fact of Western life was that all spiritual matters could only be sought through the words of the Bible, and only the priests of the Church were permitted to interpret them. Individuals could not define God's intentions, nor could anybody question the Holy Book and its definition of the universe, how and when it was created, and humanity's place in it.

The Church had brought back Aristotle to squelch the rumblings of the spirit world, to be used as the litmus test for truth and reality. So if you wanted to challenge the Church, you would now have to refute two interpretations of reality: the one as written in the great book of scriptures, the Bible, and the other as written in the great encyclopedias of Aristotle. Challenging Aristotle was considered even more intimidating than taking on the Bible.

So the Church adopted Aristotle and appropriated his intellectual arguments. Now it had power over the human body, soul, and intellect, thus making it unthinkable that a mere member of the Church, let alone any person outside of the Church without any formal education, could question the Bible, its words, and Church dogma.

In a society where education was strictly enforced—and limited to a select few—and where truths were now being defined by the Holy Book and Aristotle, who could stand up in the "court of reason" and refute these teachings and truths? Who had intelligence enough to follow Aristotelian logic, except those who had studied it at religious institutions of higher education, owned and controlled by the Church?

It is in this light, and with the Church as a backdrop—exercising complete control over a land and its people, physically, intellectually, and spiritually—that we begin to understand and appreciate how great Galileo was, for not only was he a pioneer in his field, he was also a revolutionary.

Galileo was not like Bruno, who was proclaiming mystic revelations to be visions of universal truths. He was proving things mathematically, and that made him all the more threatening. Like Bruno before him, Galileo believed in the Copernican heliocentric theory that the earth revolved around the sun, and humans were not at the center of the universe.

But unlike Bruno, he used mathematical formulas to prove the theory to be true. Galileo was the first modern thinker in the West to clearly state that the laws of nature are mathematical. Nobody had ever represented a greater threat to The Church's authority because he was questioning its truths and proving them both to be wrong—and he did it by playing by their rules!

Even though Galileo's investigation of physics brought with it great knowledge, his method of investigation did not conform to the epistemology or the philosophical investigation into the causes of things as advanced by Aristotle. At the time of Galileo, it was said that the Church kept more to reason than scientists did. But Galileo knew how to play by the rules, and he did that by attacking Aristotle's authority, which he did by promoting experimentation and mathematical construction of scientific ideas.

He did not believe in the forms, the essences, and the ideas as proposed by either Plato or Aristotle. He believed in the language of mathematics—the language of triangles, circles, and geometric figures, the language of facts—not abstract ideas and theories. This got him into trouble not only with the Church, which by now was Aristotle's greatest defender, but also with scientists. Galileo's discoveries had opened up another world, a world far beyond the teachings of Plato and Aristotle, and, indeed, far beyond the teachings of the Bible and Jesus, too. No wonder they put him in prison. Galileo had opened up a world in which new divisions were implanted in the West, divisions between science and religion, divisions that would never be bridged. When Galileo supported Copernican theory and proved beyond a doubt that Earth revolves around the sun and not the other way around, he not only dared to question Church authority, but he proved it wrong too!

It was unthinkable, unimaginable. A sacred teaching is sacred because it is absolutely true, because it is God's truth. The absolute cannot be wrong; otherwise, it is not absolute anymore, and God is wrong, which is impossible. God cannot be wrong!

With Galileo, not only do we get a person of tremendous courage and intellect, who dared to take on both the Church and Aristotle, but we also get the first inkling of the schism that would go on to separate religion from science, body from mind, matter from spirit, and humanity from heaven.

Galileo is considered the father of modern science. But he was much more than a scientist; he was actually Westerners' first great liberator—and first great revolutionary. The life of Galileo and the scientific breakthroughs that would follow in his wake completely revolutionized Western humanity's perception of reality, as well as its mentality and its lifestyle.

With the passing of Newton a hundred years later, science—the third born—would be firmly embedded in the culture of the West, along with the Church, the first child. The second born, spirituality, would officially die.

Any further esoteric attempts to gain wisdom by searching inward and any spiritual quests for the meaning of life by way of deciphering a secret code of life—the Tree of Life, for example—or in finding the sacred—the Holy Grail, for instance—would eventually be abandoned or go underground for centuries.

CHAPTER 12

THE LAST ALCHEMIST

*I*saac Newton would be the light to free the West from the darkness and ignorance imposed on it by the Church, and he would do this by discovering nature's laws, distinct from God's laws.

Newton became best known for his discoveries of motion and universal gravitation. Like Bruno, he believed in a immanent world, a world that is simple, clear, and ordered; a dynamically organized universe that could be understood by the intellect; a world that had been created—designed—by a clockmaker, so to speak, who operates more along unemotional and universal principles than along emotional and interventionist ones.

Newton redefined physics. All one had to do was look at the laws of causality, motion, and gravity, and one could understand everything. It was so simple, just like looking at a clock. If you can understand where everything fits, then an understanding of the world and how it operates at every level is also possible. All you have to do is connect the parts in the right places and then let them do their own thing.

The scope of his discovery was awe-inspiring. He had taken physics away from the level of sensory experience, theories, and ideas; away from the duality of Aristotle and Plato (ideals and essences); and away from the world of relativity, to the world of reason and mechanic predictability.

Newton's natural law and his theory of mechanical physics brought an understanding of the world down to the level of simple reason, making the world—and reality—accessible to everybody. Everyone could understand these principles, and nobody had to look for essences and forms in things anymore. Reality was no more an idea or an abstraction; it was observable, identifiable, and provable.

There was no longer any need to follow the procedure for identifying the four causes as argued by Aristotle to justify a thing's existence. Indeed, the four causes had become irrelevant and obsolete overnight. Galileo questioned Aristotle, but Newton killed Aristotle for good.

There is nothing behind gravity, no form and no purpose. There is a previous (material) cause and effect of that cause, but that is all. If we can understand the previous cause and its origin, we can know the effect because the law of gravity and motion will set in motion predictable results.

But for the other causes, there is nobody designing one thing or the next; there is no form or essence or any ultimate purpose for anything. The design of the natural laws is the purpose, but it is not a personal purpose, rather a universal and impersonal one. God, the clockmaker, has crafted the clock. Now He is no longer needed and gets out of the way.

Everything is self-sustaining; it will take care of itself on its own, naturally, in accordance with the natural (physical) laws already been set in place by the Creator. What more is there for God to do? He has done His job; now it is our turn to do ours in terms of discovering what He has designed in a "mechanical and physical" universe.

The laws are always the same, regardless of where you look; they always follow the same principles of a three-dimensional reality. All you have to do is teach people the right laws and principles, and everybody can come to know the truth—know the facts. These principles are available to all people to discover, and they allow all people to pursue their own aims, equally and without prejudice in this life, not the next.

By pursuing these principles, people can perfect themselves with their own rational and intellectual powers; they can also use these rational and intellectual powers to correct injustices and eliminate evil. There is nothing outside of these natural laws, thus nothing outside of people's scope and breadth. All that is required is that people use their intellect and apply the laws universally, rationally, objectively, and scientifically.

Armed with this new concept of Newton's—the concept of a singular cause as it applies to nature and its natural laws, and how everything works just like a machine—every physical and social field of his day picked up on his principle of physics and tried to implement it in their own field. As a result, the lessons in history became inconsequential.

Instead, all that is relevant now is looking at everything as if it is a machine and identifying all the parts as they react to each other, which means looking for and identifying the previous and singular cause carefully, unemotionally observing the symptom, and then applying the right remedy based on an objective and rational analysis.

Apart from the physical and natural sciences, Newton's principles would be picked up and applied by medicine, political systems, economic systems, and even the fields of sociology and psychology, just as long as everybody abided by the principles of the natural and material laws in a three-dimensional reality. They were even picked up by the Church!

Though Newton's discoveries would go on to become universal laws of nature, he warned against using them to view the universe as a machine. He was addressing laws of nature, not nature, because in nature, there are also immaterial laws and causes.

Like Plato, Newton was concerned with what links the material to the immaterial. He urged people not only to look at the gravitational pull of the planets and gravity, but also to ask what set the planets in motion, i.e., what pushes them and what keeps them organized.

Newton was not a religious person. He did not adhere to the Church's view of a transcendental and personal God who sits in heaven administering to all of creation—its every movement, every cause, and every effect, as well as every thought, every deed, and every reward and punishment of humans. He believed the laws of physics would take care of all that, rationally and impersonally.

But Newton was a very spiritual person. Indeed, he was as much an alchemist as a scientist. He has been called the last great alchemist in the West and the last magician. Like Bruno, he believed in an immanent God, not a hierarchical God, and also like Bruno, he believed there was a pure substance, which he referred to as ether.

He claimed that ether was the vital force that sets things in motion, a kind of invisible spirit that transmits forces (acts as a bridge) between particles. It is what pushes things; it is the cause of the movement, the force, and it is what keeps everything organized.

He believed that this invisible force—or spirit, or chi—can act over huge distances and is responsible for keeping life organized. But his peers, and later scientists, criticized him for his esoteric beliefs and for bringing "occult agencies" into science. They ridiculed him, his ideas, and his beliefs.

The Church, ever bent on surviving, had little problem adapting to the material-world reality posited by Newton, since the clarity and simplicity of science as it started to emerge after Newton was seen as a superior alternative to the spiritual ways that were gaining ground around Europe. But it would never go along with his esoteric formula.

To combat the so-called emotional and metaphysical thinking and the mystical elements of Christianity, the Church accepted Newtonian physics and rational thought, and like scientists of his time, later rejected his more esoteric ideas of ether and spirit. This is one of the most important nonevents in the history of the West.

Thus the spirit world was no longer admitted in either science or religion, and neither was able to use the spirit, or intuition, to gain insight and knowledge.

Newton would be considered the last alchemist in the West, and scientists would reject his theory of ether and go on to look at material causes as the underlying nature of reality. For all intents and purposes, esotericism in the Western world would die out, at least in so far as science and religion were concerned.

Thus the bridge that Plato referred to, linking the world of heaven and the world of Earth and the spirit world of Bruno and Newton—was now irreversibly severed from Western humanity. These so-called esoteric ideas died with Newton as did alchemy and any spiritual approach to science.

With the birth of science, Westerners would begin to look "out there" into the material world of things and, using mathematical formulas, focus more on their intellect and the external world. With intellect and its analytical capacity, they would delve into the physical causes of phenomena and discover amazing things.

It came at a great cost to the West, too. For in the process of searching the material world for truth, Westerners began to distance themselves from the immaterial and spiritual causes that are born from within. They also began to shun the intuitive world and the world of wisdom, which help one immediately connect to that inner world, the world of spirit, and give one a connection to heaven and a sense of oneness. As a result, the fall of Western humanity would be hastened.

CHAPTER 13

DEATH OF AN OLD WAY

*O*n the surface, one could argue that it was the Greeks who initiated the West's break from heaven, not science. After all, if we look at Plato and Aristotle separately, we notice how they separated reality into two seemingly different and irreconcilable worldviews: this world and the other world. In actuality, though each differed dramatically in their philosophy as articulated in their theories of ideas and essences, neither of them ever advocated that humans should separate from heaven in order to realize those ideas and essences.

They were both discussing a process of discovering reality—not an "ultimate" reality—separate from and outside of humanity. With divinity as a given, both of them were simply arguing how it manifested in all living things in nature and how humanity, as part of nature, could go about attaining it.

Plato's reflection on an eternal ideal broke with conventional Greek wisdom that maintained that humans were comprised of many gods. His philosophy was a way to explain how that eternal ideal in humans was to be found through and in nature, by becoming one with it.

Plato's ideal form of God was too transcendental and otherworldly for Aristotle, but he did not deny the existence of an eternal idea, as advanced by Plato; nor did Aristotle ever argue that humanity was outside or separate from that idea. Rather he was more concerned with how that oneness could be perceived in the manifestation of things through their essences and potentials in this world.

For him the unmanifest was no less real than the manifest, and humans were no more outside of nature than the acorn is outside the shell. For Aristotle, everything in nature was seeking its natural balance and harmony within nature, not outside of it.

Aristotle did not see the world as a chaotic, random collection of atoms, nor did he see it as a machine as is typically seen in today's world. Instead, he saw it as an environment where each thing, with its own unique essence, could seek its final purpose and realization. That is why there is order and not chaos in the universe: because everything is striving to realize its purpose.

In this case, the final purpose of a human is the adult just as the final purpose of an acorn is the tree. But different from the tree, the human's purpose is not only to have the frame and structure of a human body but also to have an understanding of what it means to be human.

For Aristotle, to be human meant to have a philosophical understanding of who you are, where you came from, how you got here, and where you are heading. Humans are here for a reason, which is to find out why they are here. Thus, gaining wisdom is their purpose.

In other words, finding our reason for being *is* our reason for being.

The purpose of life for Aristotle was not in examining the nature of things per se, or having knowledge of them because when you are examining nature, you are living your nature; hence, you are realizing your essence and purpose in life simultaneously.

Seen in this light, the purpose of man, according to Aristotle, is to attain wisdom. And the pursuit of wisdom will bring happiness, not because you are seeking it, but because you are doing what you are meant to do, which is finding out who you are and why you are here in the first place.

Plato and Aristotle were not the only Greeks to affect Westerners' perception of reality for close to fifteen hundred years. Ptolemy also greatly influenced Western cosmology. His astronomy, which was presented in geocentric models, was universally accepted until Copernicus and Galileo overturned his theory with the heliocentric model. His astrology was also accepted for an equally long time.

With this way of perceiving reality on a cosmological and astrological level, everything in the sphere above the moon was perfect and unchanging, and everything below it was imperfect, impermanent, and constantly changing. At the center of this cosmology was Earth, and humanity, as the highest form of Earth's inhabitants, was viewed as God's greatest creation.

Christian theology developed against the backdrop of these Greek thinkers: Ptolemy, the architect of how things were seen cosmologically, as an interaction of spheres or circles, with Earth at the center of his model; Plato, the creator of heaven, or the other world, and the world of eternal ideas and perfection; and Aristotle, the proponent of the four causes and the essence of things in this world.

With this Greek and Christian perception of reality, the universe was viewed as a rational universe, established or created by an entity, or God, that is all powerful and all knowing, and who does not move but resides in a fixed location called heaven. This unity of existence—above and below—gave humanity a sense of continuity and belonging; it also gave it a sense of meaning and purpose.

So in this sense, the simple (historical) teachings of Christianity were combined with the basic metaphysics of the Greeks to give Westerners a sense of purpose and an intellectual grasp of who they are, where they come from, why they are here, and where they are going. Humans were at the center of the universe gaining wisdom, and everything neatly fit in this rational and unified way of perceiving reality.

But all of this would begin to change and fall apart with the arrival of science in the West. Galileo would confirm Copernicus's heliocentric theory to be true, and suddenly humans were no longer at the center of the universe.

As a result, the Greek paradigm died, and a new paradigm was born. People started to look outside of nature and separate from it—heaven existed outside of nature and humanity outside of nature. Earth and heaven came to be divided into two distinct and separate spheres, or realms, and humans lost their holistic connections.

Before the ascension of science, it was unnecessary to question and understand nature because God was always there to protect and guide humanity. Things could never get too far out of control or too chaotic. But with the arrival of science—and everything seen in materialistic terms—people started to doubt nature's reliability and goodwill, and instead they looked to her with apprehension and fear.

Death, associated with the dark forces, and with the earth and nature, became contrary to life, rather than an inevitable stage and necessary condition of life, and it had to be resisted at all costs. The best protection against nature—death—was domination and control over it.

The dogma of this new way was that knowledge is more important than wisdom, and this knowledge should be based on evidence and experimentation. Intuition—the most common currency of wisdom—is no longer an acceptable way, since it does not speak the language of facts, logic, and rationality.

At the same time, Aristotle's four causes have been jettisoned from the perception of reality in the West; modern science is not interested in observing nature with preconceived notions about what it should and shouldn't be, and what should be and shouldn't be found.

Thus, with the arrival of science, a unified reality of life comes to be sacrificed for a way to gain mastery and dominance over nature. In the process, art, artificiality, and man-made values will come to replace the so-called natural and eternal ones, thereby resulting in a split between the sacred and the profane, heaven and Earth, and life and death.

Facts will determine reality, not essences, potentials, and ideals. What is real will be proved; what isn't will be dismissed. No gray area will be accepted anymore, no paradoxes allowed. Science is all about knowledge and absolutes, and when the Greek paradigm dies, wisdom dies along with it. And a materialistic and artificial world is born. When Bruno refused to renounce inspiration, i.e., the spirit in scientific investigation, he was burned at the stake. Since that time and up until the time of Einstein—when his great discovery came to him in a dream—no other scientists in the West dared, or were permitted, to invoke the spirits or the spirit world for their investigations into the nature of truth and reality. Thus their investigations were exclusively relegated to the material world of phenomena.

The scientists" world, the world of matter, would become one sphere of influence in the Western world—the physical and secular world—and it would be controlled by science. The other sphere, the religious world—the world of faith, the world of the Holy Spirit (not the spirit, as that had been banned)—would come under the domain of the Church.

The spirit that helps an individual to get a glimpse into the ideal and helps connect him or her to the real is the part of a human responsible for bridging the gap between the mundane and the supramundane. It is the essential link if an individual has any expectation of getting back to the source and, for all intents and purposes, die. Thus, there would be nothing to connect one world with the other any longer, nothing to integrate the outside with the inside.

Gradually, Westerners' link to the other world of Plato and the bridge that links humanity to it (the spiritual world) would be severed. Westerners would come to be educated and conditioned in a dualistic and materialistic world, creating a dualistic and materialistic mentality outside of and separate from heaven.

PART II

MAN SEPARATES FROM NATURE

… A distinct division between the mind
of man and the mind of God is drawn and we see Western
man setting out to control Nature. In the process, he
declares his independence from Heaven and begins
separating from his body and from Nature
—and the Kingdom of Man is born.

—Lama Nicholas

CHAPTER 1

THE KINGDOM OF MAN

*I*n Christianity the relation between God and humanity is constructed in essentially hierarchical terms: God is above like a king of humanity; humans are below like subjects or vassals. Basically, what we see in the rise of Christianity is the elevation of God at humanity's expense; not only have people fallen, as Plato maintained, but they are ruled over, denuded of a will, and made submissive while down here, too.

Plato's belief was that humans once belonged to heaven but had fallen from the other world because they had wanted to come back to Earth to relive their desires and ride the Dark Horse. (He also believed heaven was not a concrete place—a material place, so to speak—but a spiritual place beyond matter and the world of illusion.)

With Plato, although there are two worlds—a world we came from and the world we are in—every one of us has the free will to return to the other world if and only if we can get off the Dark Horse and escape the material world, which blinds us to our soul and our divine nature.

But with Christianity, we get humans coming to Earth because they are condemned here by God. Heaven loses its spiritual dimension and becomes a concrete and material place, the home and residence of a personified God. It becomes the Garden of Eden, with concrete things for concrete individuals, and humans are no longer free to choose to go there on their own. Heaven becomes a real and material place, which humanity has fallen from—not because of people's desires but because God condemns them here and they are already sinful. So after the fall of man by the condemnation of God, humans can never return to the "lost paradise" without the will of God.

Salvation, therefore, comes exclusively through the grace of God, not through the efforts and will of humanity. Although there is a City of God, humanity for all intents and purposes cannot enter it by its own merits, nor by its innate virtues, but only by the free gift of God. Humanity is condemned, unless saved by God.

According to Christianity, the individual is only an individual personality; he or she has no direct link with God or the universe, and there is no internal spirit to bridge the gap. Each person is completely dependent on God's benevolence; all is outside of the individual, and the individual is dependent on heaven for assistance.

In this sense, people have no rights, no free will, and no power, materially or spiritually. They are completely at the whim and fancy of God, regardless of what they do or don't do. What happens to them depends on God, for better or worse.

In effect, a person becomes an indentured servant to both the Church and God, since he or she has little say over any aspect of life—in this world or the other—in matters temporal or spiritual. Instead humans are ruled in the same way a king of an absolute monarchy would rule over his subjects, completely at the mercy of the sovereign. In ancient dynasties and kingdoms, when the oppression of the king/emperor went to an extreme, the people eventually revolted and established a new—and more representative—ruler. In the same way, after more than a thousand years of oppressive rule, Westerners felt a similar tyranny, and they revolted as well.

They saw their God above and Church below as extreme and full of spite, anger, and jealousy; hence, they were unpredictable and vengeful, offering no guarantee whatsoever that humanity could ever enter the City of God, despite all its faith, dedication, and devotion.

They wanted something more approachable, something that better represented people's wants and needs here on Earth, a world where they could exert control over their lives and not be at the whim of either Church or heaven.

They wanted a human kingdom. Maybe they would never get to the City of God above, so why not create one below? Westerners decided to get more certainty and control over their lives and turned their attention to earth; they were determined to build the Garden of Eden in their own backyard.

Now instead of being at the caprice of God and nature, Western humanity started thinking of mastering nature on its own. People would do it by imitating the heavenly God and standing outside the world, yet creating and destroying it the way God did, with knowledge and power. In this battleground, and with the feudalistic mentality as a backdrop, Descartes set off to prove that people could stand on their own two feet without the help and grace of God. Like others, they still aspired to reach heaven, but they had no desire to wait around and depend on God's grace to get there.

Descartes found one thing that could help people liberate themselves from God, which was innately human: intellect! Even though God does not divulge to all people the ways that lead to heaven, they naturally have their own innate intellect by which they can find their own way and learn the truth.

Descartes considered all thought and emotion entering his mind as having no more truth than an illusion or dream, since it could never be proven to be factual. Finally, however, he found one thing at least that he could not doubt, that is, himself. "I think, therefore I am," or "I doubt, therefore I am." That is an indisputable fact!

For Descartes, thinking was the essence of self and the proof of existence. It is the only thing one can prove to be real. Even the body, its senses, and its feelings cannot be proven that way; nor should one even consider them in evidence. Thus, the self—the "I"—becomes the real, the ideal, and the good; all else has an unreal status.

According to Descartes, everything in this world can be doubted, but the I cannot be doubted since it is doing the doubting. Thus, everything in this world may be false, but the I must be real. This was a direct assault on the Church, which would have long-term ramifications lasting until our own times.

Plato had maintained that everything on the planet was an illusion, save the soul. According to Plato, everything is in a constant state of change, thus ephemeral and not permanent or real. Humans could know what is real only by merging their soul with the eternal ideals, not the earthly and sensory ones. Descartes, on the other hand, maintained that everything on the planet is an illusion, unless proven by the intellect to be factual, hence true and real. Thus, humans and their intellect—not God and not our soul—would now determine what is real and not real.

In order to find both his way and the truth, without a Church interpretation or divine intervention, Descartes determined to accept nothing as truth—which he did not know, for a fact, to be true. In this sense, he rejected as absolutely false all ideas and opinions in which he could have the least ground for doubt. Of course, that included the scriptures and the teaching of the priests!

He no longer trusted the world as it was anymore; he did not even trust his senses. He surely didn't trust the Church; nor would he trust some words from an ancient book.

If anything has to be trusted, it has to be proved to be factual, thus real and true. It has to be indisputable. That would be Westerners' new credo, and science would be the new language by which they would articulate this new philosophy: It must be an indisputable fact.

Descartes's primary aim was to give humanity a new philosophy that would allow it to become the lord and master of nature. This philosophy, if realized, would contain the fundamental principles of all divisions of human knowledge and would give humans the fulfillment, both intellectual and practical, denied them by the Church and God. In so doing, a distinct division between the human mind and the mind of God is drawn, and we see Westerners setting out to control nature. In the process, they declare their independence from heaven and begin separating from their body and from nature—and the Kingdom of Man is born. As a result, Westerners would begin to split from heaven and the Church, but they would also begin to separate from nature as well. By drawing on an ontological distinction between body and mind, Descartes irreversibly split Western people in two, and he inadvertently created a new jailer—called I/ego—and with it they officially started separating from nature in the West.

When Descartes first uttered those famous words, "Cogito, ergo sum," he thought he was making a case for the objective and rational intellect—hence proof of existence—different from the emotions and senses, or the mind, which were feeling, transient, and relative, or unreal.

Little did he know at the time that he would become so central in getting people to separate from nature and split their body from their minds. The process birthed the concept of I and the belief that it was somehow independent and permanent and, thus, absolute and real.

In this human kingdom, people are only "really" connected to the world of ideas and thoughts that can be perceived with the intellect, which is separate from nature and their body and, more importantly, separate from their intrinsic nature—their soul.

CHAPTER 2

A MONSTER IS BORN

*I*n the chronology of the West, we now see the arrival of a new brand of thinkers, those who believe that nature is intelligible and manageable and that the Kingdom of Man can be greatly expanded by humans and their reasoning minds. With this belief, these thinkers teach the people of the West to make logical, objective, and systematic investigations and experiments in natural science in order to get power over nature—and heaven.

For the first time, Westerners make a concerted effort to get more knowledge of nature, not to be one with it but to have control over it. Now people would have to be outside of nature in order to examine and rule over it.

According to Descartes, most so-called knowledge—for instance, Plato's ideals, the teachings of the Church, or speculative philosophical writings like those of Aristotle—is not real knowledge at all; it's just conjecture. To gain real knowledge, there must be information and facts, which are analyzed by an objective, independent, and doubting observer.

In his attempt to discover hidden truths, which were in many cases concealed or simply forbidden by the Church, Descartes set up certain criteria and standards to distance himself and others like him from the controls, censorship, and dogma of the Church. He did this by proving that knowledge can come to individuals too, not only to the Church, and it can come to people better through gaining as much information as possible and interpreting it with reason and intellect.

Descartes believed that reason alone could make or enable men and women to learn eternal truths. He was opposed to sensory experiences and dreams (or mystical revelations like Bruno's), regardless of how noble they were. He saw them as a potential source of relativity and illusion, hence doubtable.

For him, a rational pursuit of truth should doubt every belief about reality without exception. For him, there is a truth, but it could only be gained (much like Plato before him argued) without any sensory experience. Reason alone could be the vehicle to truth and knowledge, and of critical importance, this could only be done independently and outside of the body (which is controlled by the senses).

Thus, according to Descartes, by conducting tests in a systematic and empirical way, and analyzing them in an objective, clinical, and logical way, people could come to understand and know the nature of phenomena as it is in fact, not in theory. That is real knowledge. So they did not have to rely on the Church anymore for its so-called truths or its holy books; they could find them out for themselves.

Thus begins a new age in the West, the age of science and dualism and the birth of a New Man. From now onward, Western humanity, through science, would start to turn its attention away from heaven and ethereal considerations, and away from nature and natural (sensory) considerations, to reason and objective interpretations. No more would the heart/soul hold sway over an individual's interpretation of reality, nor would purpose factor in. Only the intellect and its objective analysis would be admitted.

The object of the New Man's pursuit in the West is now turned away from innate virtues like love, mercy, and righteousness, and away from introspection, to the acquisition of wisdom toward knowledge, power, control, and external achievement. Power is now considered good, and to be in control—to have mastery over nature and its resources, its creatures and its people—is considered the rightful and just destiny of humanity. So what we see is the creation of metaphysical dualism and a great divide in the West, in which the substances of the human body are distinguished from the thoughts of the mind. They would essentially become two disconnected halves.

This critical distinction would never be resolved and would lead to a mind-body split in the West, since the two substances in the materialistic and rational systems are independent of each other and irreducible like the psychology of the mind and the physiology of the body. This is different from the original teachings of Plato and Aristotle, both of whom were seeking to instruct people on their true nature and how they should adapt to nature. The new way of thinking to emerge in the West taught the New Man to strive for a new way, an artificial way—one in which all that is bad and ugly in nature is converted into the good and the beautiful by humanity.

The individual becomes the creator, and his or her way is to create an artificial world separate from nature.

Thus a new vision begins to emerge, one in which the soul and wisdom are buried, and knowledge and man-made constructs are elevated to divine status—a state that teaches people to strive for the fullest and the richest of all human experience, a state that finds people split between mind and body, and a state that is under the governance of the I, separate from heaven and nature, and indeed, superior to both.

So with Descartes and thinkers after him, we have the birth of real knowledge and the birth, so to speak, of a new human being—an individual who is not only able to imitate God on Earth with his or her reason but who also possesses a personality and a will that are elevated to the place of God. The ethereal spirit of heaven is replaced by the spirit of the individual personality (the ego), and it is in full operation on Earth in the Kingdom of Man.

The will (of the ego) is now like an agent of God, in possession of His knowledge and His power. And the object of that will is the fulfillment of the New Man, who is controlled by an individual ego. Suddenly we see the Western world letting loose a monster.

Armed with logic and intelligence—and its incredible ability to rationalize and justify its every thought and action—the ego would start trying to conquer and exert control over nature, over fellow beings, and over an individual's own nature.

Like Dr. Frankenstein, Descartes had created a monster, and it is called the ego, and it would gain traction with the birth of the New Man.

CHAPTER 3

THE WORD,
THE PRINTING PRESS,
AND ABSOLUTISM

*A*s great as Galileo, Descartes, and Newton's contributions were to the emergence of a real knowledge and a New Man in the West and to the creation of a human kingdom, there were also significant events and inventions that got Westerners to change their focus, such as the Reformation and the invention of the printing press.

With the Reformation, the focus of northerners in Europe was dramatically transformed. Not only were they forced to tear down all the Catholic churches and build Protestant ones in their place, but they were also suddenly forced to interpret Christianity differently as they shifted away from a devotional and emotional view of the scriptures to a more literal interpretation. Virtually overnight, they were moving in the direction of perceiving reality as it was defined and interpreted by the word and a reasoning mind, and away from a perception of reality as it had been interpreted through the image and as it had been felt in the heart.

Henceforth, there would no longer be any services in Latin. Instead, the word replaced the image, altars were stripped of any idols, and the services came in the form of sermons by the clergy. The laity would passively sit in attendance and listen to the words of the pastor in their own language.

Suddenly absolutism was born, and it came out in the form of artificial values and distinctions as enunciated with the word and articulated with the language. With the invention of the printing press, people came to pursue knowledge and perceive this newfound reality not in limited numbers, but on a grand scale. As such, more and more people in the West came to define truth in terms of words and concept—and in terms of a reality that could only be interpreted with language.

In this sense, as Westerners focused their attention more on the self/ego than the spirit, on mastering nature rather than being one with it, and on knowledge rather than wisdom (which requires no words, only an intuitive understanding of oneness), they turned away from nature and toward the artificial means of obtaining knowledge, such as with the written word and the printing press.

At this point, the word and not the image becomes the Westerner's greatest symbol of truth, and the word and what is manifest replaces the symbol and the unmanifest. Thus, it is with the word that people come to separate themselves from a natural and holistic and cyclical interpretation of life to an abstract and linear interpretation of life. (And they start using and cultivating the left side of the brain instead of the right side.)

Now, instead of being connected to life, experiencing it personally and directly with the body, and viewing humanity holistically as part and parcel of nature in oneness, people came to see reality and its world outside of and separate from the body, as well as on paper [later on screen and on video], on the brain, and in absolute terms.

People would not have to experience reality directly anymore; it was enough to see it in words or numbers, and to interpret it with their intellect, which operates in the world of abstractions and has dominion over numbers and words.

In spiritual traditions, however, people do not believe the word can communicate truth and reality any more than clothes can identify who the person is that is wearing them. Clothes can be worn and words can be spoken, but neither can communicate truth and reality in the absolute, only relatively.

Accordingly, there are two dimensions to reality: the manifest and the unmanifest, the one we see and the one unseen, the known and the unknown. Language can describe what is known (to the mind) but cannot describe what is unknown (to the mind).

To speak of truth with words is to limit truth and reality to a man-made interpretation, or to an artificial construct. But truth and reality don't only rest in the manifest; they also go beyond appearances, where they cannot be described. Thus neither can be communicated.

According to the spiritual traditions, human knowledge is limited to words and language, but real knowledge, since it embodies both the manifest and the unmanifest, goes beyond words and language. Language is relative, limited to one person's perspective, and as such, only meaningful to the individual perceiver. It is never a conveyor of truth or reality in absolute terms.

In an artificial age, however, we look to make distinctions with language, or we try to discover the ultimate—and absolute—form of reality with mathematics and science. But in a natural world, one understands that nature, not humanity, guides everything in perfect balance.

Grass does not need lectures to grow properly, rivers do not need sermons to reach the sea, and nobody has to teach a tiger how to hunt. Language is a way of shaping our attitudes, and a way of creating artificial patterns of distinctions, valuations, and desires; it is not the way of spirit as it began with the Reformation.

Such values and distinctions are unnatural and lead us away from the Way, to the way of duality—a way that removes us from our naturalness and leads us to artificial, not spiritual, living. This kind of living not only moves people to separate from nature, but it also gets them to separate from their greater self.

To live with the purpose of gaining perfect and absolute knowledge and truth is not only impossible, but it is also foolish. How can the mind, which is limited, find—let alone define—that which is unlimited?

Language is a tool and nothing more. It should be used to convey a meaning, but that meaning is rooted in a point of view, a context, but not a truth. If we get into the habit of using words to describe reality and truth, we will get off the Way and head in the opposite direction, which is the world of artificiality and illusion—and the world of the Dark Horse.

But that is exactly what starts to happen in the West, beginning with Galileo and Newton, taking shape with Descartes and the Renaissance, gaining traction with the Reformation and the invention of the printing press, and solidifying with the proliferation of the word and the resurfacing of individuality.

CHAPTER 4

A RESURFACING

*T*he Greek ethos was a reason-worshipped, language-based culture with a focus on truth and reality through intellect and logic. This way of interpreting reality would go on to have an enormous impact on how the people of the West would come to define their version of truth and reality.

The Greeks were focused on discovering the minute, understanding the order of the universe, appreciating the beauty of the sublime, and pursuing ontologically the Being of all being. In essence, they were not concerned with, nor would they accept the appearance of a thing. They would have to explore how and why it was.

Western mentality would follow suit.

The Greeks embraced a form of radical intellectualism, using knowledge as the one-and-only dimension to judge cosmic reality, and with the intellect in control, of analyzing. This led to an overexpansion of reason and a decline of spirituality in Greek culture.

Western mentality would follow suit.

With the arrival of the Renaissance, Newtonian physics, Descartes, and a mechanical way of viewing the universe, we see a concomitant collapse of spirituality. But we do not witness a collapse of Greek culture just because Plato and Aristotle were rendered obsolete.

On the contrary, Westerners would come to embrace a rebirth of Greek culture unequivocally, and a new era was born, especially because Greek culture was not only about Plato and Aristotle, nor was it only about reason and logic; it was about art, individuality, and democracy, too.

In addition to pursuing truth and reality with words and language, Greek philosophy had also taught Westerners a philosophy that raised the individual to sublime heights and that saw this individuality realized through his or her heroic deeds in battle and through art.

It was through doing battle—by going through adversity, by confronting death, by overcoming one's fears and self-doubts—that humanity was able to find its self. Through their conquests, which were carried out by the strength of their will and determination, the people under the Greeks were able to discover their own divinity.

In the Greek version of individual realization, humans came of age through their conquests on the battlefield, not on the farms and in the countryside. It was in the form of personal and human drama and a show of courage in the face of adversity and death that humans were able to find themselves and as a result, discover the true meaning of a soul.

It was the hero, the warrior, who characterized and defined the perfect man according to the Greek paradigm, not his loving qualities but his heroic ones. In this case, if a man were to be a man, he had to first overcome real adversity. Only then would he be able to reveal his real courage, his character, and his "immortality."

That was honor, and there could be no soul without it. One did not find one's honor by fighting a drought; one demonstrated it by fighting in wars. He demonstrated it by being a hero! Look at the Spartans!

(Later, the Americans would identify honor in terms of the valor of soldiers on the battlefield and in the imaginary, heroic, and righteous characters of Superman, X-Men, Batman, Spiderman, etc.)

It was in adversity and in battle where man could best show off the "right stuff" he was made of. Only in these conditions would a man be able to show his true mettle and define himself as a "real" man. That was his duty, and honor was the crowning achievement of a dutiful man's life.

One does not show his heroic abilities by tilling the land or meditating; he needs a war, he needs a cause, and he needs a battlefield. He needs a crusade. He needs a conquest. It was this mentality, this Greek philosophy of the individual and the need to prove oneself on the battlefield that would also come to typify the ethos of the West.

But that hero-worshipping mentality would begin to change with the arrival of Jesus and his mystic teachings. Now instead of studying what it takes to be a hero on the battlefield, people learned what it meant to be weak and forgiving, and to attain honor and courage by turning the other cheek.

The virtues of war and conquest were (forcibly) replaced by universal love and simplicity. The biggest battlefield was no longer on distant shores, but on the one within. (Except with the Crusades; habits are hard to break.) Love, weakness, and peace were idealized, not war and death. And greed and its vehicle, the individual, were identified as the real causes of human suffering.

What made this period different and what made the Western people act and behave differently during this period was that they were learning from, responding to, and following a different philosophy than the one the Greeks had taught them, in much the same way as the Chinese embraced Buddhism, which was not an indigenous philosophy but imported from another land.

It was not a philosophy based on the individual and performing acts of courage in defiance of the gods; it was an esoteric philosophy that got people to act in accordance with the Holy Spirit and the will of God— and not their own will.

In this imported version, they were subservient to God, unlike the Greek version in which humans were competing with the gods. Instead of responding to their individual desires and the need for individual self-expression and expansion, people were responding to a philosophy of love for the betterment of the weak, the poor, and the downtrodden, In turn, they were sacrificing glory and recognition of the individual.

Instead of proving their worth and value through their conquests and the manifestation of their individual will, people were proving their worth through the spirit of sharing and the sublimation of the individual to a community of like-minded souls.

Instead of following a philosophy based on causality and strict rules of physics and logic, they were following a philosophy based on miracles, which caused them to sacrifice their intellectual needs for their spiritual needs.

With the arrival of Christianity in the West, Westerners began focusing their attention on heaven and the laws of God and performing good deeds now in preparation for the afterlife. They were no longer following a philosophy that romanticized killing and human sacrifice just to prove how powerful they were. Instead they were showing love to prove that God was Love and that humans could emulate Him by acting lovingly.

But this experiment in human love and compassion, human selflessness, concern for the weak, natural living, and simplicity of purpose and intention slowly began to wane as Westerners rediscovered their roots, the ones that were homegrown and no longer hidden from their view and perusal by the Church.

With the coming of the Renaissance and science, Westerners again found Greek books, their statues, and their paintings, and they rediscovered the great Greek philosophy and art of the past. When the city-states—and later the nation-states—were born, they found the warrior again as well, and war was once again in vogue.

It was a resurfacing and a rebirth, which again brought the individual and his or her great spirit as a philosopher, a warrior, and an artist into the spotlight. They had found themselves again, and the superman and the artist were back!

From this time onward, the individual in the West would come to occupy center stage, and Westerners would pursue truth, individuality, art, freedom, liberty, the rights of man, and war—all interpreted and enforced with a logical mind.

With the collapse of Church controls and its power over the people of the West, one unified system of governance—the feudalistic one—and one interpretation of reality—the Aristotelian and Christian one—disappeared, and new ones emerged in the West.

Westerners once again started expressing their individuality and freedom in terms of building enormous structures, inventing new forms of transportation and communication, creating magnificent art, disseminating and collecting information, exploring uncharted seas and territories, conquering people, trading internationally, and modernizing their lands. And they started again to express themselves in terms of heroism on the battlefield.

The individual was restored to his or her rightful place in the universe: front and center! Just look at how Westerners started to paint and what began to occupy all the space on the canvas. Now they could turn their attention to exploring and conquering the world as the Greeks had done before them. Welcome back … Nietzsche!

CHAPTER 5

A SACRED TRUTH

$\mathcal{S}$ailing to the New World represented leaving some form of persecution or repression behind in the past and embracing new opportunities in the future. It also represented an opportunity of living a life without fear and reprisal—from either above or below.

But most of all, it represented an opportunity for the realization of Descartes's version of real knowledge, the new state, and a human kingdom. Developing this real knowledge and a new state was going to be a human experiment, created at a totally human level with human reason, and with exclusively human vision, human expression, and human dreams.

The New Man was not going to be under anybody or anything anymore; individuals were going to have equal liberties, equal rights, and equal status. It was going to be humanity's greatest masterpiece. It would epitomize the human ideal, and it would all be created for the needs and wants of the material (secular) individual here on Earth.

It would be the first truly man-made, artificially created state, without any connection, influence, or dictates from the Church below or heaven above. It was going to be a man-made conception, carried out and constructed from scratch with individuals' own ideas and goals—and willpower.

It would represent Descartes's human ideal with the highest

human-held standards. God would have no role in its construction and no role in creating the new rules and regulations. Indeed, God would have no say at all in establishing this great artificial nation, only in sanctifying it as the residency of God's chosen people.

This new state would not become a homeland for the spiritually inclined, a place for self-realization and spiritual illumination, either. But it would definitely become a place for self-fulfillment and self-actualization, i.e., a place to realize an individual's personal goals and ambitions, a place to enhance one's self, and a place to improve one's material well-being and status.

The new state would be the first real place to experiment with Descartes's creation—the self—and to prove the New Man could be God on Earth and exert power over nature in this new state.

The Old World mentality was more about carrying on the traditions of the past, by way of advancing and promoting the special interests and ideas of the powers that be, and less about opening up to new ideas and ways of thinking.

In contrast, the new state mentality would come to be defined not by carrying on, promoting, and interpreting ancient cultures and traditions, but by inventing new ones. It would come to be defined in terms of humankind's newly acquired position in the general scheme of things, not as an insignificant speck of dust but as an individual with a purpose and mission in life—as one who drives his or her destiny, not as one who is driven by it.

The new state would come to be defined in terms of the secular and scientific worlds, not by blind faith and superstition. And it would come to be defined by who and what the individual was in terms of his or her own deeds and accomplishments, and not in terms of birth and bloodlines.

But in order to become successful under these new conditions and terms, one would need to be granted free and equal rights, not in theory but in fact. In other words, all new state rights and freedoms would have to be backed up and enforced by law.

Nobody could be granted special treatment or be given any special concessions by virtue of his or her race, creed, or economic background. Everybody would have to have equal rights under the law and equal opportunity to compete for the same thing, backed up by legal safeguard and guarantees.

If the New Man was to be God on Earth, he would have to progress beyond the old school of thought, and the new state represented the place where individuals could test all their new ideas and theories, where they could wipe the slate clean, and where they could be godlike as the new state defined the word, not as it had come down through the ages.

People would have to be born anew, and they could only do that by eliminating the past from consideration and bringing in new ideas and planting them on new soil, where nothing had ever been planted before, and where the people had not been conditioned by previous traditions and older versions of truth and reality.

So in this sense, the new state would come to be defined by its new structures and new ideas, and it would come to be defined by the things that it constructed and by the people who constructed them.

Thus, it would come to represent everything that was new, modern, and man-made, and in the process, it would come to think that new, modern, and man-made (artificial) were not only desirable but right and true as well. *Progress* becomes the key word.

So when the new state authors put in place a rational, democratic, secular, and legalistic society, they were not only putting in place a new system that safeguarded and guaranteed the common people's individual rights, civil liberties, and individual property, but they were also putting in place a sacred truth.

After all, the new state had been settled when the church and state separated, when the mind and body separated, and when science and religion separated. So its creation came as no accident but came about just when Westerners needed a laboratory to prove their scientific theories and investigate the nature of phenomena without the Church breathing down their necks.

It represented the perfect place and opportunity to realize everything in a rational and practical way. It represented the perfect world for the creation and establishment of the human ideal, unencumbered by superstition and worn-out traditions that had no place in the evolutionary direction of humanity and its desire to progress and understand the underlying nature of everything. In the new state, the Church would not be interfering in political matters, either. So it would become the first secular nation, with its inhabitants in possession of an independent and free will. In this new state, there would be no central church interfering with the investigation of phenomena.

The new state also would become the first truly scientific community in the world, with real intellectual freedom. Thus its discoveries would be scientifically investigated, not manipulated or influenced by outside factors.

Moreover, it would provide free and universal education and so become the first truly free and "egalitarian" state, guaranteeing that each and every individual had the same opportunities, freedoms, and rights under the law and not those acquired by birth or influence.

The new state, however, would not become a place to float iron balloons or to ponder the imponderable. This new state would not become a place to seek the ideal in another world or to philosophize about one either. It would be about finding the ideal—and real—in *this* world. It would become a place for the practically minded, who with a flick of a wrist would dismiss not only Plato and Aristotle but also philosophy in general.

Thus, the new state would become a place to realize individual dreams and aspirations that were practical and achievable in this lifetime, in this world, and in a material way. It would come to represent a place where the New Man could reach his goals in a realistic manner, here and now. And in the process, the new state would reinvent Plato's ideal, turning it upside down and placing it here in this world.

But, alas, there was a price to be paid for the establishment of this purely scientific, democratic, egalitarian, secular, and rational world in the new state, and it came at the expense of the spirit world. After all, with the creation of a secular, legalistic, scientific, democratic, and rational society—an artificial world—you get the creation of a materialistic society, with all the laws, rules, morals, and institutions to bring about their fulfillment, not a spiritual one.

Everything becomes designed for the realization of those material aspirations and goals—the economic and political systems, the educational system, the type of religions practiced, the infrastructure, the moral governance of society, and the people's values and conditioning.

Thus, the new state becomes a place to look outwardly for salvation, not inwardly. It becomes a place for material satisfaction and happiness, not for spiritual satisfaction and wisdom. It becomes a place for rational and logical expression, not for intuitive and mystical expression. And it becomes a place for sensory gratification, not for divine gratification.

Basically the new state becomes an artificial and materialistic place, where everything is created, designed, and established to help the new citizens of the world—the New Man-—find the "gold in them hills," not the spirits dwelling there.

CHAPTER 6

ENLIGHTENMENT BRIEFLY VISITS THE WEST

The Enlightenment came to the West like a crusade, but this time the crusade was not fighting on behalf of the Church, but against it. This crusade was going to liberate the human mind, not control it. This crusade would free people, not enslave them. It would do this not by the sword, but by reason, and it would come at the expense of the Church creed and dogma.

It would free people's minds by educating them; it would free them of conditioning and free them from the tyranny of dogma and superstition that kept them ignorant. It would do this by educating and informing people, not by keeping them in ignorance.

There is no history and tradition of enlightenment in the West. Indeed, until the late eighteenth century, there was not even a word for it in the English dictionary. Enlightenment has always been an Eastern tradition, not a Western one. So when the Enlightenment paid a brief visit to the West between the eighteenth and nineteenth centuries, it was not interpreted in the same way it had been interpreted in the East.

In the East, enlightenment had always been interpreted in terms of spirituality or in terms of humanity's attempt to realize its greater self by becoming one with its spiritual self, or transcendent nature.

When the lower self becomes one with the bigger self, a person "sees the light," or sees his or her divine nature and becomes one with it—becomes enlightened. In this sense, enlightenment in the East has always occupied a spiritual tradition. When it arrived in the West in the eighteenth century, it was not perceived in this way; instead it was perceived in an intellectual and rational way.

Enlightenment was seen in terms of one's liberation from nature, not in terms of becoming one with it. It was seen in terms of reason, real knowledge, and the New Man separating and distancing himself from nature—and naturalism—and getting control over it. Naturalism was old school; the Enlightenment was new school.

It was seen in terms of breaking away from religion—a way of breaking from tradition and from the past; a way of breaking from authority, especially religious authority; and a way of breaking from nature, which most Westerners associated with naturalism, hence superstitious traditions.

The Age of Enlightenment was primarily an intellectual movement that grew out of the West from the middle of the eighteenth century to the mid-nineteenth century. It emphasized intellect, reason, and individualism rather than emotion and tradition, and its purpose was to reform and develop society using intellect and reason.

It had no use for tradition and challenged any ideas grounded in tradition, grounded in faith, and grounded in religious principles. It was a movement that was adamantly opposed to superstition and intolerance, both of which were viewed as products of the Church and primitive man. Instead it promoted the advancement of knowledge by way of scientific methods, individual innovation and creativity, and intellectual exchange. Its purpose was to reform society using reason, challenging ideas rooted in tradition and in faith, and to advance knowledge through science, skepticism, and intellectual thought. It was going to facilitate humanity's final coming to Earth, and it would be realized by the New Man's mind in a new state, and on an intellectual and rational basis, not a spiritual basis. This could only happen if people were free to exchange and disseminate ideas.

The period of enlightenment flourished in the West until the early nineteenth century, when it would eventually give way to the Industrial Revolution, materialism, artificiality, and modernization. But while there, it would make an indelible impression, especially upon the political and social culture, the birth of a secular society, the creation of the major tenets of a new paradigm soon to emerge, and the subsequent evolution of Western culture and mentality.

But like everything else in Western culture since the time of Galileo, and its dualistic way of approaching reality and truth, the Enlightenment would take on two forms that we can generalize today as the American form and the European form.

The European form would be more moderate in its view of enlightenment and as such would not want to radically break from the past and old traditions. Instead it would attempt to reform and accommodate old systems of authority, old systems of power, and old systems of faith.

It would not break from them; rather it would attempt to renew and invigorate the old ideas and traditions by way of critical thinking and review. In other words, the European form of the Enlightenment would attempt to bridge the old with the new by making them relevant and useful in the present—without challenging the structures, institutions, and authorities already in place. The Americans would have no such interest or sensibilities. They were not about bridging; they were about breaking and severing ties with the past and worn-out traditions, not in reconciling them. Thus, the American form of the Enlightenment would be more radical—a form of separation and change, or as they might see it, the one of progress.

Their form would not only become the new and dynamic one, but it would also become the righteous one. The American version of the Enlightenment would end up breaking from the past, breaking from authority, and breaking from European and ancient traditions.

This form would represent democracy, racial and sexual equality, individual rights and liberties, full freedom of thought and expression, freedom of the press, eradication of religious authority (both in the legislative process and in education), and a full separation of church and state. Everything that Europe was not! It represented the future.

The Enlightenment movement, however, would not last long in Europe, or in America. Eventually it would give way to the Industrial Revolution, modernization, materialism, romanticism, idealism, science,

Nietzsche, two World Wars, violence, and a new way of perceiving reality, accompanied by the powerful and contradictory influence of religious absolutism and fundamentalism.

But before the sun set on the Enlightenment in the West, it would be pertinent to say that it was very instrumental in shaping America and leaving its lasting mark. It led to the creation and development of a secular and democratic society, protecting individual liberties and freedom of expression. In other words, it would go on to become a cornerstone of the newly emerging paradigm of the West.

In the process, however, it would cement Westerners' dualistic and conflicting perception of truth and reality as articulated by the contrasting beliefs and traditions of science and religion. It also would cement their perception of truth and reality, as manifested in Western humanity's expression of both, in terms of faith and reason.

CHAPTER 7

THE RISE OF MODERNITY

*W*hat are the attributes of a modern state? Historically the characteristics of a modern state have always meant, first of all, possessing a means of transporting goods on sea and on land. Thus, having a merchant navy, a major port, and a system of railways that traverse the nation, was naturally expected.

Secondly, it has meant having electricity, telegraphs, and telephones in order to connect to different parts of the country, primarily for the purposes of trade. It has also meant building up a major city where industries and people can flourish, connecting both to a concept of time like Big Ben in London.

Additionally, modernity has meant having Western medicine and a proper sanitation system, so millions of people can live and thrive in one city. Another component of modernity is having a modern style army and navy and possessing modern ways of promoting and protecting foreign trade and commerce.

The British were the first people to modernize a nation in the West. With their empire stretching out all over the world, the British effectively set the standard of modernity—which all other nations on earth would attempt to copy from then onward—in terms of science, technology, mechanization, mass production, rapid transit, international trade, urban planning, a powerful military, universities to train engineers to build the infrastructure of modernity, and doctors specializing in Western medicine.

It began when the British started conjuring up ideas to become an imperial power. If that was going to happen, they realized, they would have to possess control over the sea and land. They were able to do this by inventing a way to make cannons out of cast iron, thereby destroying all other rival fleets on the sea, and by inventing the locomotive, thus asserting control over the land.

The British merchant mentality and their brilliance with detail enabled them to expand their power on sea and land by devising precise schedules and timepieces, and it enabled them to invent machines to transport their goods across land and sea.

It also enabled them to coordinate ways of increasing productivity and reducing expenditures in time and money, and they were able to manage everything through their great feats in science and engineering. Most importantly, it got them to modernize Great Britain because, as the British learned, there can be no power and no imperial rule without modernization. But modernity has also been typified by progressive ideas and idealistic views, and how to liberate people from oppression and subjugation.

The French, like the British, also had imperial designs and visions of conquering the world. The French ways and means would be different, however, from the English ways since the French were not a nation of merchants like the English. Instead France was a country of soldiers and farmers. So their scope and focus would be different from the scope of merchants. As warriors and farmers, they would go on to be the great democrats, the great egalitarians, and the civil libertarians, and as a result, they would go on to promote justice, liberty, and communal rights.

Starting with Napoleon, the French set out to liberate the subjugated people of Europe from the oppression of Church rule and bring them enlightenment. This liberation would come in the form of popular governance, free education for the common people, the popular vote, popular rule, etc.

This effectively marks the birth of the nation-states as we know them today. They basically grew out of an antipathy toward the Church—and the political, social, and intellectual control it had exercised over the people of Europe for more than a thousand years—and a desire to liberate the individual from any form of religious dogma and authoritarian control.

It also represents a significant development in the genesis of modernity and the birth of secularism in the West, as well as its approach to truth and reality. For Westerners, there can be no truth and no reality unless humans are free to pursue both, and this can only happen without any interference or control from religions.

Due to an intense competition between the United States and the European states, scientific innovation became the way to gain an edge in economic, commercial, and political terms. Couple this with the arrival of the Industrial Revolution in Europe and the emergence of America, and we witness the coming about of the West as an imperial and industrial power.

As a consequence, we see incentives for mercantilism and international trade and industry, backed up by new discoveries in science and technology and a burgeoning standing military to protect all the interests of the West and their gains. In effect, we see Western nations becoming more powerful, more industrialized, more commercialized, and more modern.

With the British and French paving the way with the advancement of power, innovation, and modernity, we witness new ways of defining and shaping material reality—as discovered in the worlds of physics, engineering, chemistry, biology, astronomy, and mathematics—and we also witness a dramatic shifting in Westerners' perception of reality.

With the colonial powers expanding their influence around the world—and educating and proselytizing their colonized subjects with their culture, their truths, their realities, their language, their educational systems, and their principles of progress—modernity would expand far outside the West to all corners of the earth and eventually influence others on a massive scale, unlike anything else in human history.

With the unfolding of modernity and this new way of perceiving the nature of reality, we also witness the rise of a secular society with one integrated system of governance, one system of perceiving reality, and one way of educating and governing the people. This secular society would go on to incorporate the democratic principles of popular rule, equality for all, individual liberty, freedom of thought, free expression of the press, eradication of religious control from the legislative process and education, and full separation of church and state, as they were first articulated in the Age of Enlightenment.

Eventually this new way of perceiving the nature of reality would go on to condition the way people across the world think and act. This fostered the construction and propagation of completely materialistic and artificial societies run by the principles of modernity, progress, and secularism, and governed by, paradoxically, a people who were completely committed to a contrary perception of reality in their private lives. As the world begins to emulate and follow this new perception of nature and its secular approach to reality, it plunges more and more of its people into ruthless individuality, hopeless divisions, endless conflicts, and crass materialism, completely divorced from people's natural surroundings and spiritual nature.

This new way of viewing the nature of reality and humanity's place in the world ultimately causes people to abandon the natural world and its mysteries in favor of reason and truth and the pursuits of the mind unencumbered by emotion. And it employs all manner of craftiness and manipulation for the practical realization of power and knowledge.

Thus people worldwide begin to see their nature in materialistic terms and their meaning in terms of the realization of power, money, and modernity. With the gradual decline of the Church, Westerners begin to devote all their time and energy to modernization and the endless pursuit of power, progress, wealth, and knowledge.

In the process, the spirit is cut off, abandoned, and left adrift. The Dark Horse would now skew the Westerners' perception of reality worldwide, and as it does, they depart from living a natural life—divorced from their inborn nature—and destroy their spirit and form in the process. They now pursue modernization and knowledge to achieve fame, power, wealth, and even immortality.

Using Dr. Faust as an example, he would sell his soul to do so.

CHAPTER 8

LEADING THE CHARGE

*W*ith the fall of the Western imperial powers after World War II, the reigns for ruling the modern world would pass to the Americans. They would take the European form of modernity and progressivism and improve on it dramatically in all aspects, but with one major difference: the Americans would be leading modernism with American ideals and American individuality.

There is nothing uniquely American regarding individuality. All over the world and at all times of human history, we find people attempting to break away from convention and traditional forms of communication to express themselves and to think independently. In all walks of life, in all cultures on earth, and from the beginning of time, you can find evidence of individuals separating themselves from society and going off on their own paths.

The Greek sailor sailed off on his own to explore what lay beyond his shores, and in his quest, he discovered the virtues of freedom and knowledge through personal experience. From this exploration we got the ethos of character and self-discovery through adversity. In this way, the hero was born.

The Japanese samurai went off on his own in possession of a sword and a kimono and little else, and in his quest, he discovered the virtues of self-discipline and personal privation. From his wanderings and self-imposed poverty, we got the ethos of the warrior and his self-discovery through duty and self-sacrifice. In this way, honor was born.

The Chinese hermit went off on his own to live in a cave on the mountaintops to find the Tao, and in his quest, he discovered the Tao from within. In silence he found unity, integration, and oneness, and we got the ethos of harmony and self-discovery through solitude. In this way, immortality was born.

The Indian yogi renounced everything and went into the forests and mountains, and in his quest, discovered the *that*. In renunciation, we got the ethos of self-realization. In this way, enlightenment was born.

The Muslim Sufi took off all the trappings of the material world and set off in search of the divine, and in his quest, discovered emptiness. In emptiness, we got the ethos of pure love. In this way, mysticism was born.

In each example, all manifested acute forms of individuality and a passionate conviction that one had to be free and independent to make any significant discoveries regarding the underlying truths of human existence.

But what makes these forms of individuality so different from the American form of individuality is that individuality in most other examples is more or less perceived as the *means* to realize another goal that is far more important than individuality in itself. Honor, character, self-discipline, self-realization, enlightenment, immortality, and universal love are the goals, not individuality.

For the ancients, individuality was simply a means to an end. It freed them of the shackles of a constrictive society, a society that limited their scope and vision; it freed them from a hypocritical world, a world that said one thing and did another; it freed them from religious and cultural conditioning and the ignorance imposed upon them by social controls; and it freed them of things, possessions that would hold them down and pull them back from their path.

The key was to reduce, not add; to eliminate, not acquire; and to empty, not fill. But most of all, individuality would be the vehicle to ultimately free them of themselves, the true ource of all their suffering. In the American brand of individuality, however, individuality is the goal—not enlightenment and not self-realization, but (material) ego/ self-actualization.

As far as the Americans are concerned, there is not a higher and loftier goal than individuality; individuality is lofty enough. Indeed, being a true, free, and independent person is their form of the illumined and enlightened individual—a true manifestation of humanity's ultimate mission in life, one in which the individual is fully able to express him- or herself as a man or woman. Just being free to express yourself is goal enough.

But individuality is nothing more than the ego manifesting in its body form. So America becomes a place for the ego to manifest in body form vis-à-vis the realization of one's personality in terms of one's name, beauty, strength, possessions, body, power, wealth, status, fame, and family. In short, everything with which the ego can materially identify itself.

In this sense, America comes to institutionalize individuality. American individuality comes to represent the American dream—not just to own a house with land, but also to realize one's individuality through one's material possessions and accomplishments.

Different from other peoples around the world, who look upon individuality with great longing but also with great trepidation, Americans do not see any reason for fearing individuality and limitless self-expression. They simply throw caution to the wind and completely embrace individuality without hesitation or equivocation.

Thus, everything in America is designed and set up for the actualization of the ego through individual rights and personal freedoms. America is not designed to overcome such egoism and unlicensed freedoms, nor is it set up for the realization of a greater self or a higher, more transcendental purpose. It is established, instead, for the realization of individual greed and desire and the illusions that fuel both.

Thus, the American ethos comes to be defined by the people's quest for individuality and their desire for self-actualization, and it manifests in terms of one's material accomplishments here on Earth. For the first time in human history, liberty, free will, and individual rights become codified into law, converted into dogma, and institutionalized into a ruling and governing elite, with its own apparatus and vehicles of control and power. A new mentality and a new religion are born.

America becomes the first nation on earth that sanctifies the human spirit—as distinct from the divine spirit—and officially separates the works of the individual, and his or her artificial creations and deeds, from the works and deeds of nature and the assistance of the divine. As a result, it also severs any links to the spiritual world.

So beginning with humanity's separation from nature, followed by the philosophical articulations of an emerging mentality and this new religion—as well as humanity's eventual separation from itself and its spiritual nature—we observe artificiality being brought to fruition on such a grand scale for the first time in human history.

What we see is the birth of an artificial, man-made nation, one where the individual in all his or her glory rises up to occupy a nearly superhuman realm, and one where secularism and democracy are the vehicles for enforcing this belief in the sanctity of the individual and his or her inalienable rights.

America becomes an individualistic and legalistic society, established not by the patterns of nature and natural laws, or by God, but by the patterns of humans and the laws they established. It becomes the dream-come-true of Rene Descartes.

These man-made values and patterns are backed up by human laws—laws that are basically created, designed, and established with the sole intent of fueling the individual's desire to satisfy his or her senses (the mind included) and his or her need for self-actualization on earth.

This focus on individual creativity, freedom, and self-expression and its emphasis on material success—paired with the mentality of measuring one's worth according to one's possessions and status—ultimately turns America into a ruthlessly competitive society, driven by an egocentric philosophy and a tremendous need for worldly recognition.

Artificiality is now running on all cylinders. The profane takes its place in the churches scattered all over the plains, and the temporal succumbs to the rationalists and the individuals who have inherited the earth.

America becomes the symbol of modernity, opportunity, and individuality—and the goal for all those from all over the world who want to make it in this world, for all those in pursuit of success in the material and artificial world.

America comes to be defined in terms of the secular, religious, and scientific worlds, and the conflicts existing between them. It comes to be defined by who and what the individual is in terms of his or her deeds and accomplishments, thereby putting tremendous strain on family and community.

But most importantly, America comes to be defined by the individual, what he or she possesses and how a person gets it by his or her own efforts. Individual success—not liberation from self, or *moksha*—comes to define the American ethos, and the pursuit of success comes to define the American psyche, and both come to define this new mentality and the American culture.

America comes to represent a place where one can have success in a practical way and, in the process, find a happy life. But to find a happy life, one must focus his or her attention on elevating the needs of the I to heights of greed never manifested on earth before.

With the desires and artificial needs in place, America creates a system of commerce to reward such individual greed and desire, and it is called a free market society. Here all the senses can find a vehicle for their desire, and there is little thought or concern for the earth, nature, and the consequences of freeing people to utilize their desires in whatever form or way they feel fit.

American culture unleashes these desires with devastating consequences to the concept of unity and wholeness in general, and to the planet and all the species inhabiting it specifically.

Individuality and the acquisitive personality, and the ego that drives both, come to define this new mentality. All the freedoms that were built into the system to help people be creative, innovative, and free to express themsevles in a noble and humanistic way are now transformed so they can blatantly express their greed in a vulgar and selfish way instead.

Thus, America is transformed from a society that was established to help the soul to be free to a society that helps the ego become enlarged and the image of self to expand. It is transformed from a society that frees people to worship as they please to a society that ultimately worships the self and its illusions. And it is transformed from a society that let the spirit soar to one that kills it.

Americans usher in a new period, a new way of seeing reality in a creative, enterprising, practical, innovative, rational, and materialistic way. In the process it transforms the world and its people—and their perception of truth and reality—into an artificial way of living life as manifested through this new creed.

In effect, America becomes the symbol of freedom, rationalism, science, the secular world, individual opportunity, and success—as well as the de facto residence of modernity, artificiality, the ego, and the emerging paradigm—and the Dark Horse on which they all ride. Thus, Americans are not only riding the Dark Horse but they also are leading the charge.

CHAPTER 9

City versus Countryside

*A*s the new states and modernity emerged in the West—accompanied by their individualistic, rational, democratic, materialistic, mercantile, freedom-loving, scientific mentalities—and as the Church began to lose its central control, people started moving away from the countryside and into cities for greater opportunity.

We thus see humanity separating itself from nature, its natural surroundings, and the natural rhythms in a very big way. Not coincidentally, we also see people separating from the Church.

When people separated themselves from nature, in addition to separating from the countryside and their natural roots, they also separated from their more intuitive and feeling part. Instead they slowly began to embrace the rational and analytical part.

This meant that people would slowly be moving away from a world of visual representation and instinctual feeling to a world interpreted by the word and originating from the mind and logical deduction.

In symbolical terms, since the earth represents fertility and fecundity—i.e., the feminine principle—it signifies moving away from the feminine side of human nature, which is embodied in the image of the goddess and manifested in love, and moving toward the masculine side of human nature, which is embodied in the word of God and manifested in reason. The two are not accidental occurrences but actually go hand in hand: An individual mostly relies on intuition—the feminine side, his or her "yin: side—while living in the countryside, or the right side of the brain. An individual mostly relies on reason—the masculine side, his or her "yang" side—when living in the city, or the left side of the brain.

In the countryside people's survival depends on how empty they are, not on what they know but on what they feel. In order to feel right, they must reach a state in which they are free of any limitations. Only in that way, when they are silent and free of any outside influences—when they are one with the environment and without thought—can they know what the right thing to do is. It is a gut feeling, and they must be free and empty.

But when people are living in the city, they must rely on their wits to meet the needs of the fast-paced and hectic city life. To think well and quickly—which is a masculine or yang quality, or a quality of the left side of the brain—people must have a sharp mind, which requires filling and polishing it, not emptying it.

In city life one's survival depends on how much knowledge and information he or she has and how well one can use and manipulate that knowledge for personal gain. If one is to survive well in the city, one must use his or her mind, and that requires great analytical skills and acumen. In order to develop good analytical skills, one must have a broad range of input and information, and he or she must be able to separate and distinguish one from the other. An individual must also be able to make judgments and criticisms, which are based on artificially established values and rules of right and wrong, good and bad.

In this world, a person's responsibility is to fill, not empty; to know, not feel; and to have, not to be free. It all depends on how well he or she can use the mind. And a person must be, or always feel, that he or she is in control. Freedom is seen not in freedom of mobility and action without limitation, but in how much one has or owns, and limitation is defined by how little one has or how little one owns.

Stress comes about as a result of wanting things one doesn't have and fearing the loss of them when one has them. Possession is the catchword. Thus *having* knowledge is interpreted as *having* power and *having* wealth; all are perceived as humanity's great liberators.

Emptiness in city life, however, is an individual's greatest fear since it brings out the individual's greatest vulnerability, and thus brings one closest to his or her own mortality, powerlessness, insignificance, and eventual disappearance.

Wealth, power, and fame—ideals of the Dark Horse—are ideals to the city dweller, too, and can be realized by how well one has cultivated the mind and how quickly it can adapt to and respond to the needs and demands of the time. So it is important for the city dweller to have education and as much information as possible.

Ironically, however, these so-called ideals exist in connection with and dependent on social conditions, which are completely artificial and, as a result, subject to change at any time. One day an individual may be on top of the world, another day lying in the pits. For in the city life, no matter how much power and money one has, he or she is unable to find real freedom. Instead, the individual must always act in conformity with those around him or her.

Even more importantly, an individual must act in conformity with the arbitrary rules of conduct and behavior as set up by those in power. His or her ideal is a relative one and, as such, always dependent on others. In this world there can be no real freedom, only the illusion of it.

In the countryside, one is dependent on the heart, not the mind. The heart's instinct is to empathize, which it does not do by analyzing, criticizing, and judging others' defects. Instead it instinctively understands that each and every person is made of the same substance and is above artificial rules of conduct and behavior. It feels things holistically and, as a result, has great tolerance. The mind seeks to know, which it does by gathering all the facts and looking at things outside of the whole and by analyzing things in relation to the individual parts. The mind is brilliant at taking things apart and putting them back together again. It seeks objectivity and knowledge, and it easily makes judgments.

The heart's instinct is to embrace all differences. It seeks love, community, and happiness, and it understands things in terms of universal connections. The mind's instinct is to take things apart—to separate and to isolate. It seeks power, knowledge, and recognition. The heart's instinct is to put them together. It seeks unity.

These two environments- city and countryside- require two sets of contrary and even opposing temperaments. One requires flexibility and adaptability; the other requires order and control. One requires understanding and openness; the other requires structures and rules. One requires empathy and harmony; the other requires values and distinctions. One requires the heart; the other requires the mind.

When living in the countryside, one cannot depend on one's reason since nature is anything but predictable and dependable, and it moves outside the purview of humans' rational way of seeing things—i.e., it cannot be clearly analyzed, planned, and programmed according to their artificial, three-dimensional concepts of time, space, and matter.

To be sure, time, space, and matter exist in the countryside, but they exist as natural forces of nature, which come and go according to patterns and conditions, and which are often outside of humanity's understanding and control—outside of humanity's knowledge.

Living in nature is living a paradox, where opposites are not only in plain view for all to see at all times—and where they are not separate or isolated from the other—but also where they are interdependent and must coexist in harmony and balance.

To live and survive in the countryside means going with one's gut feeling, not one's head, and it requires that one mostly functions on an instinctual level. One goes with the flow, which means he or she does nothing but what is appropriate at the time. One adapts, one is spontaneous, and one is part of life with all its mysteries.

Living in the city, however, requires a completely different set of survival instincts, as one is not adapting to the forces of nature anymore but rather inventing and imposing one's own forces as he or she goes along. One is constantly creating new ways of achieving his or her goals, which usually entails developing more rational rules and codes of behavior in order to enforce them.

The individual is unable to adapt well since he or she is unable to do nothing and just let things be, and there is little or no spontaneity and mystery in life. The city person is always on the go and as such never able to surrender to the forces of nature and fate, unlike his or her countryside counterparts

Instead one thinks that he or she—and nobody else—is the architect of his or her own destiny. In order to carry out this philosophy, the individual is forever busy doing something and being in some way productive, especially in ways that he or she can realize personal ambitions and earn a lot of money in the process.

The city person is always looking for new ways to invent, organize, order, and control. He or she needs to know, since knowledge is power, and so is always on the lookout for more possibilities to further his or her knowledge and thus reduce the fear of a future without both. The city dweller is always doing something.

And nothing frightens this person more than the thought that he or she is not in control, that he or she is not doing something.

CHAPTER 10

NOTHING LEFT
TO CHANCE

*W*ith the rise of real knowledge, modernity, secularism, and individuality in the West, accompanied by the decline of essence and spirituality, philosophy also dies a quiet death. Speculating about the nature of reality, how, and why are no longer admissible in the newly formulated principles of science, which are constructed around logic and abidance to scientific criteria and method.

Now nothing is left to chance, and there are no longer any accidents; there is no mystery, either. Instead, all knowledge must be based on evidence and experimentation. Any description of reality must incorporate in a plausible way the reality revealed by science.

Neither heaven nor God can have any say in determining reality any longer. Any account of the nature of knowledge and the way it is arrived at must apply to science if it is to be credibly accepted.

With the rise of science, we witness the decline of traditional authority like the ancient kingdoms and religious experts. Truth, and not what they say in terms of tradition or scriptures, is to be established by methods that exist independent of them. The question of God's existence or not becomes a matter of faith, not of truth.

In the process of this existential upheaval, people begin to question the nature of their beliefs, even their natures. For example, if the movement of all matter in space is subject to mechanical laws, what about us? Is there no such thing as free will? Is everything in life predetermined, even our lives? If there is a scientific explanation for all physical phenomena, even our existence as in evolution, what need is there to believe in anything? Why even waste our time on morals and ethics? Indeed, what is the point of anything?

When Descartes declared, "All science is certain, evident knowledge," he also rejected the possibility that any knowledge could be probable. For anything to be real and true for him, it had to be "perfectly known and about which there can be no doubt." Even probability is no longer admissible!

In this new world, the world of real knowledge, the New Man, the new state, modernity, reason, Descartes, and science, material and mechanical laws rule all phenomena. That may be palatable if we consider these laws in terms of inanimate objects, but these exact sciences that were created to dominate and control nature are now set on humans.

The human body comes to be considered a machine, too, like a well-made clock. As a clock or machine, the human body can be stopped, taken apart, repaired, and put back together. In the process of mechanizing the body, the mind is separated from it. We see this split coming about when we hear Descartes say, "There is nothing in the concept of body that belongs to mind; and nothing in the mind that belongs to body."

This mechanistic philosophy of science inspires mass production in industry and mass medicine and health care, and a new age of innovation and specialization arrives. Now only material and mechanical causes are identified and sought after. The total condition of the person—personality, emotional and physical constitution, spirit, background, geography, and susceptibility to disease—is excluded from the mechanistic model of science.

As a consequence of separating people from nature and their nature, they are cut off from the whole and any sense of connectedness, interrelatedness, and unity. Instead, we find that everything is defined in material and mechanical terms, and the world is simply considered a machine comprised of physical objects causally related to each other.

Nature is not exempt from this objectification of the universe, either. Like everything else, it is a mechanism, too—just matter in motion, waiting for humans to calculate and measure its operations. There you have it: everything is there for people to measure, calculate, and interpret—and humanize.

As the body and mind split, the world is thought of as being independent of the person who perceives it, with physical laws that determine its operations and the interaction of all its parts. Humans are outside of the world, and nature—in the same way as their minds—is outside of their bodies.

In the process, science eliminates all metaphysical speculation and eventually achieves a full and systematic knowledge of the physical world, which we are separate from. Now everything is to be observed and analyzed, and we see the end of destiny, chance, and mystery.

Objectivity reigns supreme. The scientist—and everybody else if he or she is to be accepted as reasonable and intelligent—must take an objective look at matter and formulate theories to explain its operations. In this new age, we only know what we perceive and what we can prove to be true. All else is unreal or superstition.

We may assume, or our faith may want us to believe, that there is a separate reality out there as Plato and religious people maintain. And we may want to assume, as Aristotle and others have, that there is a god, a spirit, a soul, an essence, and/or a purpose causing us to feel what we do or act the way we do.

But since we can never engage them directly and prove their existence, they cannot be considered real in terms of scientific standards. In other words, unless it is material, with a mechanical causation, and it is proven scientifically to be a fact, it is very simply not real; it is a figment of imagination.

Science no longer looks at things in themselves, such as my essence or myself; it only looks at the structure and systems of phenomena and how they operate like the structure of my body and the operation (the neurology) of my brain.

This is the dawn of a new age, an age of innovation and specialization. It is the dawn of reason, objectivity, and utilitarianism. It is the rise of artificiality and man-made definitions of reality.

Humanity no longer needs the help of the muses and spirits to guide it; science will do everything now. Nothing is left to chance in this emerging paradigm.

CHAPTER 11

MAKING THE WORLD
A BETTER PLACE

To justify humans giving up their spiritual connection, science portrays the compromise along utilitarian lines and the material and humanitarian benefits that will accrue to them over time by sacrificing that connection. What we get in its place are tremendous material and humanitarian achievements, and modernity, as well as the science of ethics and the science of morals, otherwise known as utilitarianism.

The purpose of utilitarianism is to bring scientific certainty to morality and ethics. It promises to reduce or eliminate moral difference and to resolve the most persistent ethical dilemmas.

It assumes that the scope of morality is to make the world a better place. Accordingly, if we can scientifically assess several possible courses of action to determine those that will have the greatest positive effect on the world, we can provide a scientific answer to the question of what we ought to do.

In this regard, utilitarianism maintains that morality is about producing good consequences, not about having good intentions. In order to produce good consequences, we should do whatever will bring the most benefit—i.e., intrinsic value—to all of humanity. Whether or not it is actually good is unimportant; what is important are the benefits to humanity, usually measured in terms of statistics.

Moral scientists have a simple answer for the purpose of morality: Morality exists in order to guide people's actions in such a way as to produce a better world. Consequently, the emphasis of utilitarianism is on the results or consequences—the effects—not on intentions. And those effects must be demonstrable in terms of making the world a better place, such as better housing, better nutrition, better education, etc.

In order to demonstrate those effects materialistically, we see mathematics and ethics coming together, since all consequences must be analyzed and assessed in terms of numbers.

For instance, when calculating any specified action, we must determine how many people will be affected, negatively and positively, and how severely they will be affected; and we must make calculations for all accessible alternatives. Based on the calculations, we must choose the action that produces the greatest overall amount of utility. We use mathematics to do this.

Using this mathematical equation, utilitarian analysis must, first of all, take into consideration the benefits to the greatest amount of people and, secondly, calculate costs. Then it must multiply each factor by the number of individuals affected and the severity of the effects.

But how does ethics factor into the formula? How can there be a science of something that is by nature immaterial? Indeed, how can we even know, let alone measure, the intrinsic value to humanity?

Ethics, by definition, means custom, habit, or character. But it has usually been associated with defining the ideal human character, e.g., in terms of human ideals as described by Plato and human goodness and sincerity as articulated by Aristotle, and by human principles and righteousness as associated with Confucius. Morality, in contrast, normally attempts to describe whatever is good, right, or proper.

Goodness, on the other hand, refers to our inner impulses, actions, judgments, and duty and how they adhere to that which is intrinsically moral. The key words are *that which is intrinsically moral*. Seen in this light, people have an intrinsic nature, which is naturally good and moral. All they have to do is bring out that inherent nature.

Taken together, ethical and moral behavior and goodness would constitute a way of life, meaning the way of character and honor that manifests through moral and virtuous living—i.e., through a life governed by an individual's sense of principle, righteousness, and love.

Thus, the ideal human is defined, first of all, by an innate or intrinsic understanding of what is right and good and, secondly, by his or her conduct and the way he or she naturally puts that intrinsic knowledge into practice, by acting lovingly and righteously.

But without any intrinsic sense of propriety and virtue, how can one know this? Where is that innate understanding coming from? How can one know what is right and good if there isn't a preexisting "knower"? If we feel it, it isn't known; it is perceived and felt. If we think it, it isn't known; it is thought to be right. To know something, we must be one with what is known, not outside of it. And the only way of being one with something is by being of, or part of, that which is known.

In the past this came about by connecting with one's spirit or soul, or one's essence. Since the nature of the spirit was considered a manifestation of God/the Tao, it was naturally considered good and moral. In this way, we must connect with it by bringing out our own soul or spirit; in other words, by connecting to our essence. In so doing, we would live a virtuous life and, as a result, naturally be good and moral.

One would not have to think about what is right or feel what is wrong. Nor would one have to obey the law to be good. One would do what is right because he or she is right and good; such is a person's intrinsic nature. As a consequence, there is no other way to act. By acting in this way, one could never be wrong or act wrongly.

One's conduct is not contrived or manipulated out of fear or guilt by religions, or under punishment of law in the secular world. Nor is it analyzed (by the mind) in terms of self-interest as in utilitarian terms. Rather, it is motivated by nature (one's intrinsic nature) itself, and as such, there is no other way to act but the good and right way.

One inherently knows what is right and good because one is by nature right and good. All one has to do is unify with that nature—the essence within—and one will always obey the inner voice by manifesting his or her virtuous living. That is one's nature because one's essence is good and virtuous. And as a virtuous person, one can only act virtuously.

Virtue is the key. Without virtue, how are we able to distinguish between right and wrong? Indeed, how are we able to distinguish between human and beast? Virtue is the material manifestation of soul, the divine manifesting on earth. Virtue is what makes us good, respectful, righteous, just, courageous, understanding, tolerant, and loving. Morality is man-made, but virtue is a gift from heaven.

If we are in possession of virtue, it distinguishes us from other animals. Without it, we are the same—or worse.

But ever since the rise of science and secularism, ethics in terms of character and an intrinsic nature (essence) has been thrown out the window and replaced by the science of moral duty. It is no longer of any great importance or meaning that an individual defines what is right and wrong; science and society will do that for him or her. But it is important that the individual performs his or her duty to ethics.

Just as Western medicine begins taking over the knowledge of the human body and what makes a human sick, science and secularism begin taking over the ethical world and begin determining what is right and good for people. The individual is no longer responsible (or relevant) for his or her body or moral behavior; there are doctors, scientists, and lawyers to see to that.

It is important, however, for a person to live a moral life; otherwise, social order would break down. But how can you do that? How can you make a person moral? You cannot force someone to be good or moral. You can force a person to obey a law or an army, but you cannot make him or her be good, kind, loving, courageous, just, tolerant, respectful, or truthful. Those qualities have to come from within.

Only the individual can determine those values and attitudes. But how is he or she going to determine those without an essence and virtue? If one cannot intrinsically know what is right and good, how can one intrinsically know how to do what is right and good?

So with the goal of making the world a better place, we see the death of essence, along with virtue. After all, what is the point of virtue in a strictly material world, a world outside and separate from nature? How do we get individuals to this point of obeying that which is unenforceable—like loving behavior—in a world bereft of essence, innate qualities, virtues, and ethics?

Without an essence anymore, without an inner voice speaking and monitoring one's actions and behavior, and without any intrinsic sense of goodness and virtue, how can one know what is right and good, let alone do what is right and good?

So now we witness another aspect of nature that comes crumbling down: the innate, intrinsic, natural goodness of humanity, along with its essence, virtue, and intentions. It is no longer important if a person is intrinsically good (virtuous) or not; it is only important to control the outcome of his or her actions so we can make the world a better place.

CHAPTER 12

THE EROSION OF CONSCIENCE

The fundamental imperative of utilitarianism is this: Always act in the way that will produce the greatest overall amount of good in the world.

Producing the greatest overall amount of good does not mean, however, that your actions must be good. In other words, it is not imperative to *be* good, since you might have to do something bad in order to produce the greatest amount of good—like using drones to kill terrorists and killing innocent civilians in the process. Collateral damage is justified as long as it produces the greatest overall amount of good.

In principle it is bad to kill the innocent civilians, but since the bombing produces the greatest amount of good (as defined by those who launched the drones), it is justified. The emphasis is clearly on consequences, not on principles.

The technocrat pulling the trigger on the drone is asked to set aside his own (moral) principles as he distances himself from the minimum utility (the few, or many, civilian casualties) to maximize the utility (the greater good of the nation). What's best for the country trumps one's personal convictions.

Practically anything can be justified along utilitarian grounds. As people distance themselves more and more from nature, and as they come more and more to analyze everything in utilitarian terms, they also come to distance themselves from taking any personal responsibility for their actions.

In the process of defining everything in material and utilitarian terms, and abandoning any personal responsibility for anything that happens to him or her, the individual will also come to abdicate control over nature and his or her body and mind to the experts in these respective fields.

Thus, people will eventually consign moral and ethical issues to the religious leaders and social experts like priests, politicians, bureaucrats, policy makers, and technocrats.

But what about a conscience? Without virtue and an intrinsically good nature, one cannot have a conscience. One can have feelings; one can even have feelings of guilt. For example, one can feel guilty about doing something right and good for oneself, such as buying something he or she really wants but doesn't need.

But a conscience is traditionally used not in terms of feelings of guilt but in terms of feelings about knowing the truth. Conscience is what you refer to before doing something; guilt is what you feel after doing it because you feel that you have done something that you should not have done.

Conscience resides within the intrinsic nature, or the soul. Without a soul, an individual cannot know the highest standard by which to measure and compare. The soul and its expression (conscience) give the individual a way of measuring his or her conduct and comparing it with the best and highest standard of goodness and propriety in the universe.

Conscience is a built-in capacity that allows humans to sense and know ["without knowing"] the accurate thing to avoid doing. It is an inner guide that all humans have, or should have. Conscience turns up in almost all religious philosophies, wisdom paths, and spiritual teachings.

It is generally recognized to be that aspect of our intrinsic nature (soul/ spirit) that is our source of goodness, our virtuous intentions, and our inner voice. It keeps us on the straight and accurate path, known as "being true to yourself," and otherwise known as the spiritual self.

This is not truth in an objective, narrow, and absolutist sense, but it is truth in a subjective sense, where we are living our life moment by moment from a solemn awareness of our self as spirit, not form. When guided by our conscience, we are aligned with our truth, which really means our true nature or our trueness. This is our essence!

With the arrival of science, however, essence, conscience, and virtue disappear, since feelings are not quantifiable and accurate. Utilitarianism replaces it with logic and reason, and we witness the gradual erosion of conscience on a grand scale.

CHAPTER 13

STANDING ON THE SIDELINES

*F*rom the dawn of science onward, people in the West have begun to find themselves strangers in a strange and hostile land, reduced to their material components and structures, with no rhyme or reason for being here in the first place, save the impersonal laws of the physical universe. So how are they able to get back "home"? Indeed, without the spirit to guide them, how can they even know there is such a home out there?

By the end of the eighteenth century, Newtonian physics has been embraced in the West as the new reality, and everything comes to be defined in terms of a mechanical way, with a mechanical causation. Now everything in life happens because of a prior cause and condition or because of a cause and effect (what Aristotle called efficient causality).

So in a huge departure from the old Greek and Christian paradigms, when things were defined in terms of four causes, there are now only two causes to consider: the preceding cause and the subsequent effect. The other two, the essence/form of a thing and its purpose, are discarded.

In other words, things happen for reasons that lie in the immediate past, not goals or purposes that lie in the future. In one fell swoop, science not only strips Aristotle of his intention and purpose, but it strips humans of their purpose and intention, too!

To repeat, according to Aristotle, if you want to understand something, you have to identify why it is here and where it is heading. But according to science, you only have to examine where it has come from and where it is "programmed" to go.

In this way, science essentially frees itself of Aristotle and his four causes by arbitrarily deciding that it is not necessary to identify immaterial causes, i.e., a thing's essence and potential. Instead it directs its attention to examining a thing's material constitution—in a logical, methodical, and systematic way—without any direct connection to what it is examining.

However, by looking at things in an impersonal and objective way, science lost the ability to talk directly about what it was analyzing. This detachment took humans away from the spiritual world of reality and a direct way of knowing something personally—what Plato called the "bridge to the divine," or an intuitive way of coming to know truth.

So science moves away from intuition and wisdom and probing and looking to answer the big questions, such as who we are, where we come from, and why we are here, to the direction of knowledge and making the world a better place materially, here and now.

Thus, the final cause, function, or purpose—for a thing or for a human—is no longer part and parcel of the investigation. You examine the actual way in which something happens, not *why* it is happening. Gone is humanity's purpose for being here. Gone is the soul, and also gone is the mystery and the spirit.

This is the Newtonian view, and it would go on to form the core of Western mentality as articulated in the newly emerging paradigm of the West. Whether you consider the state of an economy, the nature of disease, the nature of society, or human psychology, you look at everything in the same way as you look at a machine, trying to identify how it is actually happening.

In other words, you look at the motive but not why one has the motive or where it is heading because it has that motive.

The Aristotelian paradigm states that an object seeks its natural place within the universe, humans being no exception. The Newtonian paradigm states that an object remains in a state of rest unless a force acts upon it. In other words, it is going nowhere unless forced to go somewhere by an external agent. It reacts; it doesn't act.

With the arrival of science, we see people acting with no overall purpose or final cause. Impersonal forces, not divine ones or destiny, bring about change; the universe is pushed, not pulled. It is the past and not the future that determines what happens.

Everything and everybody in this universe is determined by the same mechanical and material forces; each is a product of its/his or her past conditioning. Nothing is going to a place or direction because it wants to find its natural place in the universe or because it is destined. It is going there because it has to go there; it is being pushed there.

It has no choice (seemingly no will, either), since it has already been determined because of what has already happened. It must go where it is going because everything must follow the mechanical laws of physics [cause and effect] with no exception.

Aristotle's view was not the only view to suffer a fall. The Church's view of reality also suffered irreversibly with the advances of science. For example, if all movements of matter in space are known to be subject to the mechanical laws of causation, what about humans and our bodies? What about things at the micro-level? Can they be exempt? If not, how can one argue the existence of a God and His effect on humankind?

Moreover, as explained by science, if everything can be examined, what need is there to believe in God or heaven anymore? Apart from the emotional and a childlike psychological relief that believing in a higher force gives us, what scientific reason is there to maintain a belief at all? In fact, how can one even speak about morality or ethics if everything—even our evil deeds and immoral acts—are already predetermined?

With the arrival of Newton, his physics, and science, the world and everything in it is reduced to a mechanism in motion. Humans are merely standing on the sidelines waiting to calculate all that has happened outside and independent of what is happening in their world. In this way, they are no longer a part of nature and the world; humans are observers, independent and outside of nature and the world.

As a result, any and all presuppositions—notions about essences, forms, virtue, goodness, souls, spirits, gods, or whatever—are forever cut adrift. There can be no prior element in scientific knowledge, no outside and immaterial factors operating outside the mechanical laws. There is just one singular and previous (material) cause creating one singular (material) effect.

Thus, with the arrival of science and the creation of a new paradigm, metaphysical (and philosophical) speculation becomes a moot point, and humans set out to obtain a systematic knowledge—and control—of the physical world.

All matters relating to the so-called immaterial world, whether it is spirit, intrinsic nature, soul, or God (essences and potentials have long since been forgotten), are relegated to fiction. They are not admitted into the classrooms of reason, rationality, and science; they are not admitted into the church pulpits of faith, either.

Science instead begins to focus on structures that govern people, the physical entity—i.e., an individual's physical structures, genetic structure, chemical structure, biological structure, psychological structure, etc. But in looking at the structures of humans, science would also distance itself from nature and the human spirit and why we are here in the first place.

In the process, humans would begin to lose touch with the immaterial world, the world of spirit, the world of soul, the world of mystery, and their own inner world. They would instead come to identify themselves exclusively in terms of material and artificial makeup and identity, and they would come to see themselves as the measure of their physical and material needs, not their spiritual ones.

In this way, the concept of balance and harmony that one gets from having three legs, not two, would be lost in the West. Instead the edifice on which the paradigm of the West would come to be erected would end up having only two legs and two sides, not three. We now start to see the unfolding of absolutism, imbalance, opposition, conflict, competition, and disharmony.

Over time, the Greek and Christian paradigms would collapse completely, and Westerners would switch their focus from the inside to the outside, from wisdom to knowledge, from the future to the past, from the natural to the artificial, and from the kingdom in heaven to the Kingdom of Man.

This would find full and complete expression in the newly emerging paradigm of the West.

PART III

MAN SEPARATES FROM SELF

Over time, and after much conditioning from the paradigm of the West, we have come to repress our natural instincts and treat them as enemies of the real me. Instead of feeling connected to our body and its nature, we start to think from the head and do what we think is right for the real me. In this way, we come to live outside of our bodies, outside of nature, and most importantly, outside of the spiritual self.

—*Lama Nicholas*

CHAPTER 1

THE PARADIGM
OF THE WEST

*E*verything depends on a point of view. A point of view determines how we perceive reality and how we define what is real. In fact, a point of view determines our destiny, since we are products of our beliefs, which give us a direction in life. In other words, we become what we believe. But our point of view is rarely our own; it is conditioned by the culture we come from and the education we receive there.

We do not spring out of thin air as individuals with points of view; we spring from the soil in which we were born and nurtured. And in that soil are planted the values and beliefs from which we take to be real and self-evident truths. We rarely, if at all, question these values and beliefs because that is the side effect of growing up in a particular culture, our conditioning.

But in actuality, these values and beliefs are paradigms, propagated by a society in order to maintain social order. There can be no social order without control, and that control cannot be maintained by physical means alone. Thus, a society must propagate values and beliefs that are transmitted from one generation to the next if it wants order, and these are passed on by the prevailing paradigm.

Paradigms are sets of assumptions, concepts, values, and practices that form a view of truth and reality for a large group of people that shares them, especially since assumptions, concepts, and values are taught, usually in schools and, as a result, form a collective way of thinking, or mentality, of a people.

This mentality, which is rarely questioned or analyzed, intersects with a culture and determines how people in a community parent their children, how a nation governs its people, and what beliefs and values it instills in its people from top to bottom, from beginning to end.

If it were only a custom or tradition, perhaps it would not go on to have so much influence over so many people, their countries, and their cultures, since they can become ritualistic. But a paradigm distinguishes itself from a custom or tradition for precisely this reason: because it does influence a people, their values, their belief systems, and their cultures. Most importantly, a paradigm affects a people's mentality and its perception of truth and reality.

Regardless of which culture a people grow up in, the paradigm rarely is challenged. People, like fish who cannot see outside of the waters where they swim, cannot see outside of the culture in which they have been brought up. As a result, they find themselves unable to question their values and beliefs because they are products of their conditioning.

Unless we are able to fully realize how completely we have been influenced by a paradigm—in our case, the paradigm of the West—we can never fully understand that the beliefs we hold as our own, our points of view, are actually a result of our conditioning through this paradigm and not our own unique way of interpreting truth and reality.

The principle concepts that characterize the paradigm of the West and run through almost all aspects of life in the world today—from science and politics to business and medicine—are the Descartian mind-body schism and the Newtonian mechanics and the dualistic, materialistic mentality they both foster. More than anything else, these two concepts have influenced our perception of reality and the way we define our lives in dualistic and materialistic terms.

Although this mind-body split can be attributed to the Greeks, Descartes is credited with creating the scientific divide between the mind and body. The separation was initially required to allow science to continue exploring the physical universe, without being accused of challenging the domain of the Church, which included the mind and the soul. It is has become embedded in Western culture ever since.

Added to this separation, the discoveries of Isaac Newton further accentuated this duality as manifest in the paradigm. Newtonian mechanics have formed the indisputable foundation of physics for more than two hundred years.

When taken together, not only do we see material duality in full view and perceive the nature of reality in macroterms but we also see that Descartes and Newton have influenced how we perceive and treat reality in microterms. For example, the Newtonian model of the universe sees everything in terms of mechanics. Because of this way of seeing reality on a macrolevel, the human being is also considered in terms of mechanics – but on a microlevel.

Therefore, in Western medical science, humans are perceived more as machines, not living organisms, and so most treatments for their illnesses consist of material cures, such as chemical interventions, surgery, or technology. Nonmaterial remedies are either not understood or simply not allowed.

This perception of reality—that everything can be identified in terms of mechanical and material laws—has created a culture and mentality that believe everything can and should be interpreted and fixed by biological and chemical means, modern equipment, and high technology.

In the meantime, taking responsibility for one's community, one's welfare, and one's health and wellness—as well as taking care of oneself in terms of nutrition, disease prevention, and exercise; healthy living habits; calming the mind; and self-healing—have been deemphasized, discarded, and ignored.

The basic belief of the paradigm of the West centers on the assumption that material improvements and proper education will make people happy. Happiness is the goal as is eliminating our material privation and our ignorance, which, it is assumed, are the reasons why we are not happy.

For example, if an individual is poor, it is best to look at the political and economic systems and ways to eradicate his or her poverty. In the same manner, if an individual is uneducated, it is necessary to look at the educational and social system and ways to eradicate his or her ignorance.

The assumption here is that people cannot be happy while they are either poor or lacking in a proper education, or both. And the best way of improving their condition is by eradicating the previous cause of their suffering and replacing it with a superior (materialistic) version. In this way, people can be happy.

It's a search-and-destroy formula at every level and in every facet of life, one in which you must identify the material/external cause of the suffering, root it out, and finally destroy it. There is no concept of balance and harmony in this formula, only an aggressive and militaristic form of conquest, since by eliminating the opposition you can be in control.

You don't live with the problem; you kill it. This is one of the most important beliefs of the paradigm of the West. People can be happy if, and only if, they have successfully eliminated the previous cause of their unhappiness, that is, the material/external cause of suffering. Only in this way can people be in control of their lives, and only when they are in control of their lives can they be happy.

The Western paradigm also believes that certain material and mechanical (Newtonian) laws define reality, not spiritual laws. And as such, humans must use their reasoning (Descartes) mind to understand them, which means they must be educated enough to know what reason and rationality are.

So if people hope to be happy—and happiness is the key in this paradigm, not spiritual enlightenment—they must then, logically speaking, not only improve their material conditions but also their wealth and their education (rational and scientific), and not be under the whim and caprice of nature and superstition.

In order to be educated, one has to be able to think in a certain way, and one also has to be free in order to think that way. At the same time, one has to acquire a certain level of knowledge. In order to do that, one has to abide by certain intellectual disciplines and rules that the system has put in place. Naturally, educational, economic, and political systems are put in place to foster such thinking.

In this way, the paradigm of the West is backed up and supported by a new and modern state, with the attendant material systems, procedures, constitutions, and laws to foster the secular way, and people are taught how to use their reasoning minds to follow the rules and unquestioningly obey the laws.

Once the man-made, or artificial, rules are in place, people are free to improve their lives on a practical level, which they can do by asserting their individuality through industry, innovation, technology, communication, trade, and political systems that allow them free speech and freedom to move about, create, and express freely.

The enemies of the paradigm of the West are authoritarianism, ignorance, poverty, disease, political and religious persecution, conformity, anarchy, superstition, ancient tradition and custom, spontaneity, and suppression of individual rights and free speech. They must all be eradicated and eliminated; otherwise, one can never be happy.

We can see that Western mentality and the paradigm it engenders is all about improving one's condition and environment on a practical and physical level, which, it is assumed, will organically improve one's condition on other levels in the process. It is about making things better on a visible and demonstrable level in materialistic, systematic, methodical, practical, and demonstrable ways.

Naturally, for things to get better there must be a value of bad or worse and better and good. In other words, there must be a duality of opposites. So instead of adapting to adversity or one's conditions as they are now and seeing things in relative terms as only temporarily good or bad and subject to change, people are educated to eliminate or destroy one's bad conditions. That is the only way to get rid of them, by overcoming, conquering, and destroying them—forever.

So if people are from a poor country, they must do their best to eliminate poverty and the root cause of that poverty, which are the conditions that brought on that poverty in the first place—such as their country's history, their lack of "right" education, and the "inferior" and "uncivilized" culture from which everything sprang.

Why else would they be poor and backward in the first place if it weren't because of the conditions that got them there, which are their superstitious beliefs, their poor education, and their backward (traditional) way of thinking? If it wasn't for these people's poor and backward form of education and their poor and backward cultural beliefs—most of which come from living in nature—would they become poor to begin with?

So if one is going to evolve—survive in this dog-eat-dog world—to get better and to have superior physical and material conditions, one must overcome or eliminate the causes of these inferior conditions, including the (outdated) culture, religious beliefs, traditions, customs, superstitions, and ignorance.

Basically, according to the paradigm of the West, the very conditions of living in nature are what are impoverishing people and making them unhappy. Nature is the enemy! Thus, if one wants to be happy, the sources of this unhappiness—nature and one's material privation—must be eliminated and conquered.

In order to do that, one must become educated in the Western style of education, which means learning the right ways of governance and commerce, the right ways of protecting free speech and individual rights, and the right way of perceiving truth and reality. It also helps to get out of the countryside and into the cities.

In other words, to overcome poverty, one must leave nature for the artificial; one must leave behind the old and embrace the new, which means becoming educated; and one must become secular, that is, individualistic, democratic, rational, objective, and practical.

Basically, one must become liberated of old customs and traditional ways. One must become modern and progressive. Being educated at Cambridge or Harvard is the gateway to success.

For all intents and purposes, if one really hopes to improve the quality of one's life in today's world, one essentially must become a convert to a secular world, embracing its view of science, equality, democracy, freedom, governance, management, wealth, health, psychology, feminism, sexuality, modernity, and evolution—and especially its man-made and artificial ways.

To be sure, this creates a mentality that presupposes that humans are actually (not theoretically) free to improve their condition, and this can only become a reality in deed—not in word—once the right institutions, systems, and structures are in place. This includes religious freedom, a constitution, democracy, individual rights, universal suffrage, and the rule of law.

If people do not realize them (actual improvements in his or her freedom, wealth, and well-being) something is wrong with the people, not the system. It's their failure; it can't be the fault of the system. What is fundamental is the placement of the right structures and systems in order to facilitate the betterment of people's material conditions.

Of course, this type of mentality also implies that there is a linear and permanent state of better and worse, good or bad. To improve one's condition is to improve one's physical, financial, and material well-being. It means going from an inferior position to a superior position, from a lesser to higher status, and from poverty to wealth.

Like the theory of evolution, this mentality implies that going up the ladder is how one gets better and evolves. It never considers reality in terms of patterns, cycles, and reversals. We move on a straight line until eternity; the higher we go, the better off we are. A fall is not considered; there are just different stages of progress, all moving upward.

However, the paradigm of the West is not only about improving the material conditions of the social order. It is not only about secularism. If it were, it would primarily stress the rule of one class over another (or one party over another) and attempt to persuade the other classes (the other party) to accept the system of beliefs of the ruling class/party and to share their social, cultural, and moral values like it did in imperial societies.

If it were only a secularized world, as in communism, politics and economics would govern the ways and beliefs of the people, and the powers-that-be would be promoting class/party divisions and class-based social order. But politics and economics alone do not govern modern Westerners. Of equal importance is the weight the paradigm accords to the religious order.

In this sense, what distinguishes the paradigm of today from the paradigms of the past is its dualistic interpretation of reality as manifested in terms of a secular and religious society, both of which are materialistically based (Jesus did not resurrect in spirit form) and trying to make people happy by leading them in opposite directions.

For in this paradigm, if everybody is to be happy as it promotes (only a few can be CEOs, politicians, priests, millionaires, and graduates of Yale), then there must be a society in which the greatest number of its people are ignorant. Only in this way can people take the myths to be real.

A secular society can do this by promoting social and economic improvements, by convincing everybody that their vote matters, and by turning everybody into a consumer with equal rights to buy. A religious society can do this by promoting faith and by decrying reason and intellect as the perpetrators of illusion and enemies of faith. Thus, we can see how the paradigm of the West is first and foremost identified by its dualistic interpretation of reality. This mentality presupposes two things: one, that an individual has a (free) will and that its imposition on people, places, and events is always the right thing to do.; and two, that things have an intrinsic (and permanent) value of better or worse.

Thus, the new paradigm of the West, with its artificial and materialistic mentality, approaches the betterment of humanity with a dualistic mentality of either/or—right or wrong, better or worse, mine or yours—and subsequently goes on to create structures, systems, institutions, governments, militaries, schools, laws, and beliefs to facilitate this mentality.

In the process, an unwritten dogma is established through the paradigm that attempts to delineate the good from the evil, the right from the wrong, the ethical from the unethical, the educated from the ignorant, the superior from the inferior, and the rich from the poor.

It does this with a firm and absolute conviction that the New Man is actually free to do so, that this new individual is not a subject or a victim of fate and not a product of destiny, and that the individual—not God—is in control.

This mentality also has a strong conviction that things actually have a permanent and everlasting value. Moving from an inferior to a superior status means bringing better living conditions, more choices, and happier lives—forever!

This is the path called progress, and it is found in a modern, democratic, and secular society. It is manifested in the rates of higher education, increased consumption, and longer lifespans of its people, all of which are brought about by the advances of science and technology.

In today's world, most of the nations are products of Western invasion, Western commercial intimidation, Western education, and the forces and power of the philosophy and mentality of the paradigm of the West.

The method by which most nations govern their people is no longer a product of their own history, culture, and customs, but of Western beliefs and values. Whether colonized, Communist, or capitalist, all countries have been conditioned and influenced by the West, and we can observe that there is no other version of reality in the world today, other than the paradigm coming out of the West.

So what we see in the modern world—after years of conquering both foreign lands and foreign people's minds in the name of freedom, science, secularism, democracy, and religion—is that there is no other version of reality in the world today other than the Western one, and there is no other way to rule people than the way promulgated by the paradigm of the West, which is the secular, democratic, artificial, materialistic, and religious way.

There is only one way of perceiving reality and living life nowadays, and that is the Western way, with its emphasis on the new state, the New Man, and the pursuit of happiness and realizing one's dreams. Thus, if people can eliminate the material causes of their suffering and ensure an improvement of their material lifestyle, they can be happy.

Consequently, according to this paradigm, people are not happy. Not because their souls are lost—as Plato and other spiritual traditions argued in other paradigms, overcome and obscured by the Dark Horse—but because they are poor. Poverty is why one suffers, and overcoming poverty is how one can be happy.

In Plato's world, and among virtually all spiritual traditions as well, people are not happy because their souls are lost. And their souls are lost because they have become victims of desire and illusion. If people ever hope to find their way—and end their suffering—they must find a way of overcoming the power and control of the Dark Horse.

But in the Western paradigm of today, the *cure* for humans is to *ride the Dark Horse* because the cure for one's suffering is not at the immaterial or soul level, but at the material level.

In this world, the realization of happiness comes with the realization of desire. And in order to realize desire, certain conditions must be established. First and foremost are ignorance and illusion.

CHAPTER 2

AN INNOCENT
BYSTANDER

*W*hen we talk about the paradigm of the West, we are basically talking about a mentality and philosophy that takes the inhuman side out of nature—i.e., the natural, the spiritual, and the metaphysical side—and puts the human side in—i.e., the physical and material side.

In ordinary language, this would mean putting the scientific interpretation of nature and reality in and taking the naturalistic, spiritual, and religious/philosophical interpretation out. In practical terms, this means taking the theoretical out and putting the actual in. This means examining nature in terms of the actual way something happens, not why we think it should happen; it also means taking the spirit, the soul, and the essence out of nature and replacing it with the actual, the mathematical, the genetic, and the biochemical.

Because of this way of humanizing nature and looking at everything materialistically, people begin to see themselves like everything else in the physical world as acted upon by an outside and external force.

Nothing and nobody is immune or invulnerable to this universal law: Everything is operating according to the laws of gravity and causality, and as such, human life must also be influenced by how he or she is "hit" or affected by outside forces. In effect, people become passive recipients of life like a billiard ball—innocent and fine until outside forces knock up against them and invade their world.

So what we see with the arrival of the new paradigm of the West is that humans become victims of outside forces; they are no longer directly responsible for what happens to them. For all intents and purposes, they become innocent bystanders.

The individual is no longer personally affecting and influencing his or her character and destiny; rather outside forces are responsible for both. Whether those forces are behind his or her physical disease, as in a case of an external virus, or whether those forces are behind mental disease, alcohol abuse, or drug addiction, the person is the victim of circumstance.

In either case, the individual is innocent of his or her disease. So in curing a human of disease—mental, social, or physical—one must look outside for the cause of the disease, whether that cause is pathogenic, social, psychological, or familial.

Humans are no longer encouraged to "know thyself," to look inside for the causes, i.e., they are no longer encouraged to see that their own mind, their own ego, and their own desires are the root cause of all human suffering.

With this new mentality, a person's desire—past or present—has absolutely nothing to do with disease anymore, either physical or mental. Instead, it's all about external physical causes. So the way one thinks—which affects how one feels, which affects how one acts—is no longer a valid consideration in the equation of humanity and what makes one tick.

Instead of attempting to elevate the mind (the heart), as people were encouraged in ancient times and in spiritual traditions—and is accomplished by calming the mind (the heart) and reducing its desires—people begin to focus on the ego, the I, and elevating the self to godlike levels.

Now the individual starts looking outside his or her body (and heart) for the causes of disease and human suffering. The individual is encouraged to strengthen his or her ego, not to weaken it. This is done by elevating the Dark Horse at the expense of the spirit, which will suffer irreparable damage with the rise of the ego.

Humans' thoughts, which were perceived to be the root cause of disease and suffering in ancient times and in spiritual traditions, are now considered the very stuff of an evolved and liberated individual. Indeed, it is by thinking that we can be free, and it is by thinking that we can end our suffering.

So the more we think, the more we can understand. And the more we can understand, the better we are able to understand why we are suffering. In other words, the more knowledge we have, the more power we will have over nature, over others, and over ourselves.

This is the key to understanding the paradigm of the West and how it has caused humanity to separate from nature and, most importantly, from the spiritual self. The mentality that it has fostered in the process is the perception that one is outside and separate from nature and the consequent need to have power over nature, others, and one's self.

Instead of perceiving one's thoughts as the impetus behind our every deed, action, and emotion—and the cause of our character, our destiny, and our suffering as it was perceived in spiritual traditions—people no longer consider their mind and their thoughts as having any relevance on their circumstances, destiny, health, and suffering.

People are no longer responsible for their lives; they are no longer living life and creating their destiny as active and responsible participants of life. Rather, they are outside of and apart from life, victims to outside forces and outside influences that hit upon them; they are just innocent bystanders.

CHAPTER 3

THE TWIN PILLARS

To understand how the paradigm of the West has caused humans to separate from their spiritual self and how they have come to view themselves and nature distinctly and separately, we must identify the two principal pillars on which this separation has been erected: religion and science.

The Christian religious view sees humans as naturally evil. If left to their own devices, they would not become better people; on the contrary, they would revert to animal and beastly ways. According to this way of thinking, humans cannot be natural because if they are, they will just become animals, no different from other animals—wild, barbaric, and unruly.

It is therefore incumbent on the trainers, educators, and priests of society to make sure this does not happen. This they do by denuding people of their natural qualities, by "inculcating higher values," which means forming and informing people in the way these educators deem appropriate. Once they have done this (successfully stripped the individual of his or her natural instincts), they go on to construct or condition the mind.

This (negative) view of humanity is basically born from the Christian religious belief that humans have fallen from heaven—or have been condemned to Earth—because of their evil ways; humans are here on Earth as a result of this inborn and evil nature, which is brought about or precipitated by the body and its carnal needs.

Humans, as a result of their innate carnal and bodily lusts, must learn to overcome their bodily cravings, which they can best do by denying or repressing them. So, if there is any hope for humanity (and there is not much, according to the Christian religious view), that hope rests on how it is able to transcend the body and its sensual cravings so people can move on to the level of the soul and eventually return home to heaven.

In this version of humanity, Earth is an inferior and dirty place, fit only for savages and beasts, and humans, while they are on this earth and responding to their bodily needs, are nothing but savages and beasts. Put together, humans and Earth are unsavory, inhospitable, and dangerous entities, and if we allow ourselves to be seduced by either—the nature of humanity or the nature of Earth or, even worse, both—we will be thoroughly corrupted and condemned.

So if humans want to be saved from this purgatory on Earth, if they hope to be able to go to heaven after they die, they must not allow themselves to be in harmony with the world and the earth around them.

In other words, people must deny their humanity and their natural qualities, their primordial nature and nature itself. Instead, they must learn how to transcend their own personal and human needs—and the needs of nature and the earth—to those of heaven and the needs and requirements of God.

In order for a person to find salvation, he or she must not be permitted to live and act naturally, but to live and act in the abstract. In other words, a person must not be allowed to be a human. His or her proper element is not here on Earth now, but up there, somewhere in the great blue sky later.

The proper element is not when an individual is acting naturally but when he or she is acting unnaturally or artificially. The proper element is not when the individual is acting innocently or simply, in touch with himself and others, but when he or she is distancing him- or herself from the environment and those around him.

Humans must be trained and formed not to be a man or a woman, not to be a body that feels, and not to be a spirit that connects. Instead, they are to be a soul with no feelings for or connections with anybody, a soul that lives in the abstract and not of this earth, and a soul whose sole function on Earth is not to be of this earth, not to be of this body, and not to have any spiritual connection.

In this view of reality, an individual cannot be *he* or *she* anymore, but *it*. And as such, humans must be immune to any sensual cravings, any desires, any needs and wants, and any spirituality. Indeed, they must be lifeless and indifferent to life in general because it is life—nature—that corrupts in the first place.

So, according to this version, the Christian religious version—which is very much a part of the paradigm of the West—if humanity has any hope of salvation, it is not going to happen here on this planet or at any time during one's lifetime. It can only happen "out there."

It can only happen after an individual is no longer alive, when he or she is no more of this earth, no more a man or woman, and no longer in possession of spirit. It can only happen when the person is another entity, not him- or herself, and not here, but when he or she is a transcendental and an inhuman soul in another realm, lifeless and dead. So training will begin by learning to block out what people feel as humans and preventing them from acting like humans, with innate spiritual and divine qualities. The training begins by getting people to fear nature and to deny their own (instinctive) nature—the spiritual self.

The second major cause of humanity's separation from nature is due to science and its view of humanity. In this view of reality, people can only be real when they are thinking rationally and objectively—when an individual is a logical thinker, when he or she is separating the material from the immaterial, when he or she is responding to certain rules and theorems, and when he or she is deciphering formulas and equations.

In other words, humans can only be real when they are not connected to the body at all—when the intellect is different from and outside of the heart and the thinker is outside and different from the mental.

Now, since an individual is using his or her reasoning and rational aptitudes to gain real truth—not in the abstract, but real demonstrable truth, proved with facts and figures—reason and intellect are deemed not only separate from the mind and the emotions, but superior to them as well.

In this new way of perceiving reality, only those matters that derive from the intellect are admissible in evidence. Thus, only those thoughts that are constructed by human intellect are considered admissible; all else is a figment of imagination, or unreal. (Needless to say, those who are in possession of reason and logic are considered the real, and all others are the illusionary.)

As a result, what we get is a division, a separation between human emotion and human intellect. Human thoughts come to be considered superior to human emotions—and even the mind of God—since humans' thoughts, different from God's, are rational, impartial, and unemotional and can be proved to be true. In other words, the intellect (the artificial) becomes the real and all else is the unreal and illusory, including God!

Apart from human intellect, the scientific view also believes that the human is nothing but a selfish gene or an egoistic cell, whose reason for existence is to guarantee his or her own survival. In this worldview, different from the religious view, humans did not fall from anywhere; they sprang up from below, from the very earth religionists so fear and revile.

According to science, there is nothing ethereal or otherworldly about humans (the human body, to be exact); this is just the stuff of fiction and fantasy, all delusional thinking, with no basis in fact and material reality. In actuality, humans are going nowhere but to their graves, where they will naturally decompose and return to the earth and the natural elements.

Humans were born from the earth and are evolving, with no particular destination or purpose involved. They are just adapting along the way, and as they adapt, they change (because they have to in order to survive). That is it. There is no ultimate residence, no heaven, no God, no purpose, and no mystery.

It's simple, not complicated; there are no esoteric reasons for human existence—no internal struggle between a human's earthly qualities and his or her divine ones. There is no ethical internal angst, and there is no dichotomy between what humans feel and what they should feel. They feel what they do because that is what every member of the species feels. It's in the genes.

There is nothing unique or sublime about humanity. There are no values attached to it, good or bad, noble or ignoble (unlike the religionist's perspective). Only the history of the species and its fight for survival matters.

Because of this constant fight with nature (fighting is a constant theme in the paradigm of the West), humans must adapt to their environment in order to survive, which they do by mutating into different forms and developing newer, more evolved qualities to help with their survival.

This, and not a higher reason, accounts for who and what we are today. There is absolutely nothing motivating us—certainly not a transcendental entity, a soul mysteriously hidden somewhere inside us all—nor is there a great intelligence behind our creation, a designer to all the complexities of life. The only thing behind our actions is our DNA and its survival.

There is nothing good or bad about us, either, as there is nothing good or bad about being a snail, a frog, an eagle, or a cicada. Each and every creature on this planet is in the same boat, adapting to its environment and moving forward as it does, without anything or anybody behind us. There are no supportive external agents or helpers, either. Refusal to adapt is why the species perishes.

According to this version, which is a more chaotic one than an ordered one, everything seems to be defined in terms of its utility—even humans. We are nothing more than the motivation behind our genes and our cells, in a constant state of becoming. And the motivation behind each and every cell is simply its own egoistic need to survive.

That is humanity's purpose: not to become anything, not to get anywhere, not to realize anything—just the ego and its need to survive. (The reason that it, the cell or gene, or anything for that matter, has this need to survive is never explained.)

Apparently, according to both the religious view and the scientific view, humans are clearly *not* what they appear to be. They are either what they must ascend to in terms of a higher ideal, as in the religious version of soul, or they are what they must descend to in terms of their survival, as in the scientific and utilitarian version of materialism.

One version says that humans are here to survive and that they will do whatever it takes to that end. They will do whatever is deemed necessary for the welfare of the individual cell, the individual human, and the individual species. This makes humans selfish and their motivation utilitarian, since they are always acting in their own self-interest and for their own self-preservation.

The other version says that humans are here to be something higher, something that they are not already, an ideal. So their motivation is to go beyond what they are, to a higher and more evolved level.

In neither version is a human a human, part of Earth like every other creature on this planet—at one, interdependent, and in harmony with all aspects of life and nature. Humans are really motivated by factors that are outside of their body—and outside of nature—working on different levels and with different motivations from other creatures on this planet.

Humans are not attempting to cooperate, nor are they seeking to integrate the elements or to unite opposing forces. They are separating and dividing, and they are seeking independence of and freedom from nature, others, and themselves.

They are not motivated by the universal principle of harmony and balance; nor are they seeking to combine and unite the polar forces of nature. Instead, humans are motivated by competition, individuality, and fear, as well as compunction to choose one way over another.

They are not balanced or seeking balance. Rather humans seek to conquer and destroy. They act out of balance with and in opposition to nature, others and themselves.

Either people are functioning at the soul level—at an idealized level—imagining the otherworldly, or they are functioning at a mental level, analyzing their interests and calculating what is best for them in this world.

In both cases, they clearly are not functioning like the other creatures of the earth, at an instinctual level, operating and surviving with the use of the spirit. Humanity and nature are not one; they are divided. They are not made up of the same stuff but in opposition, and therefore in conflict.

When these two versions are taken together, we can understand why people would argue the need for education since we are either inherently evil, as in the religious view, or inherently selfish, as in the scientific view.

If left on their own, acting naturally and with no formal education or training on how to act, humans would either be totally corrupt or totally violent, or both. In either case, a human is a real brute with absolutely no natural or redeeming qualities, save those that are artificially and externally instilled in him or her, either by moral religious teachings or scientific and utilitarian teachings.

The main impetus behind the paradigm of the West is this religious-secular divide, and the belief that people are inherently bad and/or selfish, and the fear that if they are allowed to act naturally, they will naturally perform evil and selfish deeds if not kept under control. Thus, society needs strong laws/strong morals and enforcers of those laws/ morals.

So the thinking is that people need to be controlled, and the best way to control them—barring locking them away for life and policing them round the clock—is to educate them on the so-called right ways. Teach them the ways to distinguish right from wrong, good from bad, and me from you—basically the ways that keep people away and separate from their natural ways but connected to artificial ways, as defined and expounded by the paradigm of the West.

CHAPTER 4

THE REAL ME

$\mathcal{A}$s a result of these teachings and their dualistic way of seeing reality—outside and separate from the whole—it slowly becomes next to impossible to see things in terms of connectivity and integration. Instead, people see separation and division. In this process, and on a microlevel, they lose their ability to connect the body to the mind as they come to be treated and perceived as different and separate entities as well.

For example, *my* needs and desires—individually and collectively—are quite different from the needs and desires of the body. The body is there, and *we* are here, and rarely do the two meet, but *it* does have needs, and *I* do have to take care of *it*. Thus, people associate the body with the physical world and do what is required to accommodate its basic and daily physical needs, such as eating, sleeping, and using the toilet. The body is there to survive.

But the real me is not the one I see reflected in the mirror or the one eating; it is the one who is looking at the reflection. It is not the one reading the newspaper or putting on makeup; it is the one watching me read the paper or put on makeup. It is not the one using its senses or the one just moving about; the real me is the one who is aware of me doing these things.

The real me is the agent—the one behind the body who is doing the acting, doing the feeling, and doing the thinking; it is the one behind the doing. It is the one who is aware of being something more than what meets the eye. In other words, the real me is not the body; it is the one who is conscious, the one who is aware, and the one who is observing what the body is doing. It is the one who is orchestrating everything.

That is the real me—the person with whom I identify, the one with an identity, the one with ideas and beliefs, the one who thinks, the one who doubts, the one who is aware. That is the real me, not the body.

And the way I identify myself as a person, distinct and removed from my body—or the body of others—is through my beliefs, my attitudes, my image, my memory, my education, my culture, my wants and desires, and my dreams and aspirations; in other words, through my ego.

That is to say, everything that comes from the outside and is inculcated in me over time is considered to be the real me. That which is natural to me, such as the body and everything within it, is considered alien and unimportant.

The body is like a horse that we take to the well or a dog that we take out for a walk, but it does not possess a consciousness; I do. So it is inferior to me. It is the real me that leads the horse to the well. They are not one and the same but different, with different needs and requirements to satisfy.

In a bizarre and even sick way (what else is this mentality but a schism between one entity and another?), we come to view the body as separate from us and, in a way, not very important to us, either. Of course, it has its daily needs and requirements like all other animals, but they are at a basic level, and what is basic is considered of a lowly and inferior status.

We take care of these needs like we take care of a pet, but we don't take care of them very well, primarily because we don't think they are part of the real me—and because we don't think they are very important to us, either.

For instance, we eat for fuel and energy, not because our body has certain elemental or nutritional requirements and needs for balance. So we eat and behave as we see fit, not as is fitting to our body, its conditions and specific requirements.

But it did not start this way. As children we were in perfect harmony with the needs and wants of the body. Indeed, they were one and the same; the baby and the needs and wants of the body were inseparable.

The baby does what comes naturally, and there is nothing to prevent it from being one and the same with everything it is doing. The mind has not yet been created, values have not yet been conceived, and a way—an ego—has not yet been formed to separate the baby from what it is doing or to make it feel it is different from, or outside of, what it is doing.

The baby is innocent, and that innocence translates as unconditioned and unfiltered living and life. It is not afraid of anything, least of all life, but is curious about everything and willing to experiment with everything too. It is adventurous and spontaneous.

But that all begins to change as the baby grows and gets an education—as *it* becomes he or she; as it becomes American, Chinese, or French—and comes to be told what is right and wrong, what is good and bad, and what is real and unreal as defined by the paradigm of the West.

As the child gets more and more education, he or she slowly comes to dissociate from his or her body and natural inclinations, and instead starts to associate and identify with the mind and unnatural inclinations. It becomes personified by ego, and the real me is born.

This is where the real problems begin and how we become so corrupt, violent, and materialistic, not to mention so egoistic. It is not because we are inherently bad or evil, but because we have been *told* that we are, because we have been *taught* that we are. And since it is the body that is the vehicle of nature and naturalness, it is likewise the body that is perceived to be bad.

So we come to learn that we must suppress the body's instincts and desires. In this way we come to dissociate ourselves from our body, and the paradigm of the West facilitates this. Thus, we are no longer behaving like children at one with our body and the environment; we have become programmed and grown up, and as a consequence, we perceive ourselves as separate from and outside of our body and our environment.

As grown-ups we no longer consider ourselves children connected to our internal and external worlds. Instead we form walls and fences to cut us off and divide us from nature, our natural inclinations, and a feeling of oneness. Now we are separated from that world, thinking and feeling that the real me is separate from and superior to nature and the body. From this perspective, we start to see the body as the lower part of us, as the base and criminal part of us, and as the part that, if left uncontrolled, would either kill everything or desire everything in sight.

It is no longer beautiful, natural, and innocent like it was as a baby. Rather it is the primitive part in us, the savage part, the dirty part, and the impulsive part that must be repressed at all times; otherwise, there would be total bedlam and total anarchy, both in society and in our own lives.

Over time, and after much conditioning by the paradigm of the West, we have come to repress our natural instincts and treat them as enemies of the real me. Instead of feeling connected to our body and its nature, we start to think from the head and do what we think is right for the real me.

In this way, we come to live outside of our bodies, outside of nature, and most importantly, outside of the spiritual self.

CHAPTER 5

IMAGES AND SHADOWS

$\mathcal{T}$he paradigm of the West propagates the consumption and acquisition of external things and goods and people as the basis of happiness, and it does everything to foster the ways and means to acquire them. It does not promote that people should get control over their desires; it promotes ways to satisfy them:

A desire for wealth drives the mind to wherever wealth can be found, so why not seek out the stock market or listen to an analyst on television? A desire for sex drives the mind to find a place where the body can find sexual arousal, so why not look to the Internet or pornography, or take a trip to where you can get it easily?

The desire for sports drives the mind to the sports field, so why not go to a game or sign up for a cable sports package? The desire for God drives the heart to seek out permanence, so why not listen to an evangelist or go to a church for assurance?

The mind keeps running to fulfill its endless desires, and the paradigm of the West helps people to seek out ways of fulfilling their insatiable desires. In this way, modern humanity keeps chasing happiness, but it chases it in all the wrong directions.

True happiness does not come by realizing our desires in the external world; it lies inside, in our own self, and nowhere else. It comes by realizing our spiritual desires; it lies within the big self and whether or not we are able to reduce the material desires of the Dark Horse and bring about control of the mind. It comes about by searching inside, not outside. It comes about with self-realization.

But modern humanity does not look there simply because it has never been encouraged to do so. It is a product of the paradigm of the West, which has always stressed looking outside for truth and reality and acquiring external objects and people in order to attain happiness.

Most importantly, however, modern humanity does not seek happiness from within because it is a product of art, artificiality, and the illusions that both foster. Art is one of the most seductive ways of not only stimulating our senses but also in keeping us addicted to them; it is also one of the most powerful ways to keep us bound to the phenomenal world and the world of illusion.

Indeed, the more powerful the art, the more powerful it will appeal to our senses. If we look at the world of Hollywood, the media, advertising, marketing, and the Internet, can we have any doubt of its universal appeal and powerful influence?

This world attracts us to the temporary things in life like beauty, power, money, and fame—and it strengthens our emotional attachment to senses and desires (exactly the types of things you do not want to be attracted to if you want to weaken the Dark Horse). This world also misrepresents reality in the sense that it causes us to think the artificial world is real and the natural world is unreal.

Because of the incredible emotional hold this world has over us, we are held back from our true calling, which is to soar above this level (the level of our senses and the material world) to the timeless and nonsensory realm beyond, or to the world of spirit and the divine/Tao.

Man-made representations of reality—art and the artificial world—are the greatest risks to our spirits and the greatest impediment to humanity's quest for truth and self-realization because they represent the world of images and shadows, sense and sensibility.

In this world everything is man-made and artificial, an unreal reality constructed by humans. It's all smoke and mirrors and not in the least bit representative of the real world. Real art does not come from an image or representation; it must come naturally, void of artifice and ulterior motives of any kind.

For art to be real there must be no self in its creation, no presence of a mediating agent between the artist's inspiration and the mind into which it has come. It comes from a "selfless" self, a self with no ego, a self with no aspirations for wealth, fame, or power. It comes from an anonymous self. It comes from spirit.

For art to be real, artists must also be real. In other words, they must be empty and anonymous. They must be an altogether passive medium for giving expression to the inspiration. In this case, the creation is that which touches the artist, or that which he hears from outside, or that which flows through him or her.

For art and the artist to be real, there should be no desire and no human involvement, so to speak, just the spirit operating through him or her. Indeed, there should be no concept of art—and no artist, either!

Neither art nor life should be man-made and artificially inspired, but instead should be inspired by something that transcends the mundane. This way of creating—and living life—brings the individual into the world of mystery, in which the work of art and the person's life become one and the same. They cannot be captured and made to work by means of one's ego and intellectual analysis, or for fame or profit.

This way of living and creating can neither be taught nor attained by ordinary means; it comes mysteriously and is beyond the intellect and human reason. The work comes out naturally and without any conscious effort; it comes out spontaneously and is divorced from artificial and superficial considerations, as well as from any utilitarian motivations.

But for this to happen, one must first be in a certain state that allows this to come—a state that naturally precludes the unnatural, artificial, and superficial from entering; a state of concentration; and a state of one-pointedness and nonduality.

That state cannot come to those who are living superficial and artificial lives, or to those who are online, or to those who are governed by man-made values, greed, desire, and selfish considerations.

Basically, it can never come to those who are under the influence of the paradigm of the West and ruled by the Dark Horse, with all its sensual desires, distractions, and illusions.

That state can only come to those who are sincere and respectful, quiet and still, and to those who are reverent and have a wholehearted devotion—or faith—that enables them to reach the highest level of purity, tranquility, and harmony.

We cannot pretend to do this in a state of duality, with artifice or in artificial settings. We must do this in nature, in a state of oneness, where the spirit can find stillness and quietude, and where there will be no mind and no thought but only mystery and all the treasures of nature, just waiting to be tapped and revealed.

This is the light that spiritual traditions refer to—the light in all of us—but it is darkened by the Dark Horse and the Western paradigm's influence on us and their emphasis on art, illusion, power, consumption, and greed.

If we hope to express light, we must be *of* light. To be that way, we must be on the path. In other words, we must be *in* nature and *of* nature simultaneously. To be of nature, we must be natural, and to be natural, we must get out of the way and not let the human mind—and its artificial constructs—interfere.

We must leave things to nature and to the body of the divine/Tao, which is most evidenced in nature. It is in nature alone that we see the universal patterns and rhythms and that we also see the universal spirit manifest.

In nature we see examples of selflessness as well. Nature gives food from the soil unceasingly and unconditionally; it gives an ample water supply, continually flowing from the mountains and streams; and it gives constantly circulating air in the atmosphere—all done without profit, selfish motives, or conditions.

In nature we see justice when things decay and die in autumn and winter, we see compassion and forgiveness when things are born again, and we see harmony restored in spring and summer.

In nature we see courage in the animals, which protect their offspring selflessly from predators. In nature we see the seed give birth to the tree, the tree give birth to fruit, and the fruit give birth to the seed, which drops to the ground, and repeats the cycle. We see miracles like this in nature, and we are in awe of its wonders.

We know not how it is done or why; it is a mystery. But it is done, and it is done unceasingly and selflessly. So while living in nature, we are shrouded in mystery. The divine/Tao comes to us selflessly, unceasingly, and unconditionally, and it is there for all to take as needed—freely.

In nature we are in a world of mystery, a world that cannot be penetrated by the intellect or described by conceptualizing. It can be apprehended only by our intuition and best appreciated by our spirit. It is the ideal setting for the spirit.

The message is for humanity to be what it really is. That is our real purpose in life, and the pursuit of that purpose is the only thing worth living for- to be an integrated and unified spirit, not a fragmented one influenced by images and shadows and controlled by the desires of the Dark Horse and perpetuated by the paradigm of the West.

CHAPTER 6

BOUND BY ARTIFICE

*U*nfortunately, few people are living in nature any longer, at one with their natural surroundings and their inner and intrinsic natures; therefore, few are living spiritual lives. Instead, most are living lives day in and day out according to artificially contrived realities, rarely questioning the reality of these contrivances.

We have become so accustomed to these artificially constructed factors in our lives that we have come to consider them reality and not just conveniences introduced primarily for commercial purposes.

Take, for example, time. Instead of looking at the utility of time and how it was organized to facilitate trade, we have come to be attached to time and consider it a truth of life and not an artificially constructed concept. Indeed, most of us don't feel that we could live a meaningful existence without time being a major factor governing our lives.

There is no longer a universal acceptance of the patterns and rhythms of nature and our natural responses to them. Instead, we have learned to wake up in the dark because the clock says it is seven o'clock in the morning, even though our body says it is a different time.

Sadly we have come to let this artificiality govern our lives. It is one thing to let artifice enter our lives out of utility, but it is another thing to let artifice *govern* our lives because there are consequences to pay for abiding by artifice and avoiding or eliminating nature and its natural patterns and resonances. Utility, convenience, and imposed artifice often come at the expense of ignoring or reversing nature and its natural patterns and rhythms.

Nature is about the dynamic, constantly shifting relationships of one functional system with another, always within the context of the whole system. No aspects of the universe, the galaxies, or the solar system function as independent, discrete entities.

By the same token, no aspects of the personality or body function as independent, discrete entities. Our emotions shape our body, our body generates feelings, and our spirit affects our body. Just look at the body of one who lacks self-confidence, who has just been defeated in competition, or who has just learned that a loved one has died.

Because everything is in a constant circular motion, all process is cyclic, and everything contains its opposite. Understood in this way, one does not separate cause from effect or choose one way over another, and one does not look at truth and reality in dualistic terms. Instead, one understands that one thing transmutes into the other in a never-ending cycle of transformation and metamorphosis.

The day does not cause the night, birth does not cause death, the clouds do not cause the rain, and summer does not cause winter, but one precedes and the other follows. The chicken makes the egg, but the chicken grows out of the egg; they are only mutually generative.

Day becomes night, and night becomes day; winter becomes spring, and spring becomes summer. Rain comes from clouds but is not caused by clouds. These are cycles of nature, but they are not about time; they are relative aspects of an alternating cycle along a single chain, each one linked to and dependent on the other.

Time is an artificial concept invented by humans to make our life more convenient, like the creation of train schedules. But there is no such thing as absolute time—there is only relative time in relation to space and place, which is always revolving in cycles.

But most of us live our lives according to time and the values we attach to it, which means most of us have strayed from living our lives naturally and according to the cyclic rhythms of nature.

We have moved to living our lives artificially and according to the concepts of past, present, and future. We have strayed from cyclical, or natural, living and, in the process, have become hostages to our own (artificial) creation: time—past, present, and future. These are man-made concepts that have come to govern our lives, not just to make them easier and more convenient.

For time to exist, there must be a fixed point of departure to demarcate the actual beginning—a singular moment. And there also must be a distance and space that time is crossing in order to reach another destination. But what is the actual beginning of spring? What is the distance/space it is passing? What is the destination? How do we measure it?

There is no past in a cycle, nor is there any future in a cycle; there are only continuing moments, which are defined simply as "before" and "after." We may want to define our lives in relation to a particular moment of spring and measure it in terms of time, but it is actually our individual relation to the cycle that we are measuring, not time.

It is important to adapt to the artificial creation of time but not be bound by it. However, most of us *are* bound by time, not simply responding to cycles of time. When we are bound by time and artifice, we are bound by what is known, and accordingly, we live our lives in a habitual—and predictable—manner, outside of nature's natural rhythms and outside of its mysteries as well.

But when we are living naturally, which means living in the present, we are living life spontaneously and flexibly, and we are adapting to whatever comes our way in a balanced way. In this way life is unpredictable and our lives are dynamic, and we are living inside of nature's natural rhythms.

As such, we are alive and living life as it is, not how we want it to be or how we expect it to be in relation to past and future. We are living it independent of any conditioning imposed on us by time.

But the creatures of habit—people who are conditioned and bound by artifice—are living outside of the now because everything has become separated and isolated by the instruments of time.

That's what time does. It makes us feel outside of or separate from nature, and it causes us to focus on and identify with what is unnatural— like getting us to identify everything in life in terms of past and future, and cause and effect.

This is the basis of the paradigm of the West: everything is fixed in time and fixed physical laws. We are bound by what is fixed, and we have come to define reality by what binds us. Thus, everything is identified in terms of (predictable) causes and effects, which can only happen with time as a backdrop.

Calculating reality in terms of causality causes us to feel outside of nature and gets us to identify with what is unnatural, such as time and the events that happen in time. This way of perceiving reality steers us away from living life.

As we regulate our lives according to seasonal sporting or corporate events, we become spectators of life rather than participants in life/nature with all its wonder and mystery. We live our lives indirectly and vicariously, not personally, directly, and purposefully.

We pay a heavy price for being bound by artifice. The first problem is that it makes us feel separate from everything else and isolated from everything else. These feelings of separation and isolation create fear in us, and we project these fears, this separation, onto our world. When this happens, we create our own world to protect us from these fears—the fears of old age, sickness, and death being our greatest fears.

Thus, we create a lifestyle that will prevent those fears from arising in us, such as watching more TV and team sports, spending more time online, shopping at malls, and working harder and longer in the office.

We have found over the years that the best way to keep those fears from arising is by living a life that gives us the illusion that everything is permanent and indestructible. There is no better way of reinforcing this illusion than by habitual behavior. Thus, we become creatures of habit, not in order to live life but to keep us from living it.

We are bound by our own projection and fears, and then we become creatures of habit to insulate us from such fears. In the process, we sacrifice freedom because freedom can only come to those who are living in the now, not to those living life in the past and future. Then we complain that we have no freedom!

This is the second price we pay for being bound by artifice: we sacrifice freedom. As long as we are bound by our own fears, there can be no freedom; instead suffering becomes our constant companion.

To be free we must be free of our own fears, and the only way of being free of all fears is by living life now, at this very moment. When we are able to live in the now, we realize that the real us does not live in the past, nor does it live in an imaginary future; it only exists right here and right now.

To be free we must be free of our conditioning and habitual behavior. But in order to be free of both, we must be able to live in the now, unencumbered by our conditioning and our conditioned responses. That means being aware.

But awareness cannot come to those who are ruled either by their fears or by the responses to those fears—addictive, obsessive, compulsive, and habitual behavior. It cannot come to those who are ruled by their watches, either.

Awareness can only come to those who are not bound by artifice—and to those who are not completely conditioned by the paradigm of the West and controlled by the Dark Horse.

CHAPTER 7

THE CENTER OF
THE UNIVERSE

*W*hen people begin to think and act like this—bound by artifice and separate from body, others, and nature—we witness the rise of narcissism, and with that we get people elevating their ego to sublime levels. In this world, they come to see themselves as the center of the universe—not Earth, not nature, not even God.

Humanity becomes the reason for living; nature exists as a mere afterthought for the realization of ego. It is a purpose-driven world, driven by human ego and its individual greed, independent from and disconnected from nature.

Nature is no longer considered a conduit between heaven and earth, and as such, is no longer considered a necessary step and transition to self-realization. Humans do the realizing. Gone are the days when the individual sees him- or herself manifested through the laws and ways of nature. This is the human's domain and responsibility; nature is only there like some music in the background.

It is all something that a human does, something that he or she obtains, something gained from his or her own actions. To live in nature, to let it bring the spirit to him or her, to do nothing, and to surrender to nature's force and spirit smacks in the face of the narcissist, who is the center of the universe and in control of his or her destiny.

Humans have become the center of the universe; they are the ones in control, not nature. This is best exemplified by their use of and connection with the computer. Nowhere do people feel more in control and more powerful than when they use the computer. All one has to do is press a button and ... bingo ... somebody either appears or disappears.

The computer gives one this illusion; it gives one this illusion of being in control, of being the center of the universe. That is power, control. Can being in nature give people such power? Indeed, does nature have such power? Can it make people appear and disappear at will? Is it any wonder that so many people are on the Internet?

Who in his or her right mind nowadays would consider the human spirit in any other way than its metaphorical value? For in humans' attempt to harness and control nature, they have reduced everything to the material and demonstrable: if it can't be seen and measured, it can't be real. So obviously, the hidden laws of nature cannot be real anymore, but just something cute and fanciful to be viewed in a Walt Disney movie made for children.

People are no longer focusing on calming the mind and attempting to overcome ignorance and illusion as in ancient times; instead, they are living in total ignorance and concentrating on satiating their senses, without any self-discipline and self-restraint. People have become nothing but raw, unlicensed desire, wholly focused on perpetuating illusion and the ego is driving those illusions.

"Amaze your five senses" is the standard litany and standard modus operandi of the human lifestyle and behavior today. The five senses, or faculties, are no longer there just for the invention of tools, the creation of art, and the refinement of culture. Rather they have morphed into the objects of desires in themselves, to amaze and gratify regardless of what the expense or outcome.

Humans have created a completely artificial environment and in its wake a people who are unable to cope and adapt to nature and their own nature and essence. Is it any wonder why so many people are unhappy and sick? People are not only identifying with their senses and the objects of their desire, they are also, as a consequence, identifying with their illusion of self, ego, and the gratification of mental desires.

This transformation of the senses—and the mind that rules over them—has in turn transformed the human perception of reality. Humans have created a completely artificial environment, and its greatest offspring is the birth of the narcissist and a narcissistic society.

People have lost their roots. In much the same way that the grandchildren of immigrants have culturally little in common with their ancestral roots, modern man and woman today have very little in common with their natural and spiritual roots.

Addiction, without question, is now one of our greatest diseases, but the greatest disease of all is the narcissistic illusion of an all-powerful and permanent ego. For in the addictive personality, we have the source of many of our diseases, but in the narcissistic personality, we have the source of all our addictions.

Besides our physical dependencies—addictions to alcohol, food, sex, drugs, tobacco, etc.—we also have our psychological addictions, such as addictions to power, status, recognition, work, travel, gambling, exercise, fame, television, the Internet, computer games, videos, appearance, etc.

If we were not so narcissistic, would we have such addictive personalities? If we were aware of our spirit and not living independent of it—going through life unaware of its needs, let alone its existence; aimlessly and habitually living a narcissistic life, hell-bent on satisfying the whims and caprices of the mind and ego—would we have such addictive personalities?

In this narcissistic age, we have lost our connection to the spirit world and with it any connection to other spirits and nature. We are living totally artificial lives, which are predicated on and ruled by a materialistic and narcissistic response to needs that are physical and emotional at their root. The use of (or addiction to) food, alcohol, drugs, and sex is essentially our way of validating our existential reality, despite the evidence to the contrary.

The narcissist's reality is the belief that he or she is the center of the universe, and through addiction he or she validates that belief. The narcissist is not trying to overcome his or her addictions and the avaricious need for self-validation; nor is he or she trying to elevate the mind. The narcissist is becoming a prisoner to both his or her body and mind and the illusion that both are real and permanent.

Eventually the narcissists will come to understand that they are not what they think they are, or more appropriately, they will come to suffer from low self-esteem since other people do not validate what the narcissist thinks he or she is. Then they will look for a form of escape, which they can get through their addictions. Through addiction, the narcissists place themselves firmly back at the center of the universe and, perversely, confirm their belief in themselves.

The addictive personality brings out the true manifestations of the narcissist and his or her addiction to the illusion of ego. The constant need to reinforce that illusion—which narcissists can do by putting themselves in situations where they feel they possess power, albeit in a negative way— is at the center of the universe.

Sadly, in this age of narcissism, few people are aware that the true cause of this addictive personality is their separation from love and nature, the decline of their spirituality, and the loss of simplicity, naturalness, humility, and a connection to the whole.

Instead, this age is typified by the emergence of a narcissistic image and delusions of power and grandeur, all of which are solidified by the ego and its desire to govern the whole illusory process. And it was all set in place by materialism and the dualistic and artificial way we go about perceiving reality, as perpetrated by the paradigm of the West.

If we want to talk about humans and their spiritual nature, we must talk about one who is free—one who is free both in terms of his or her physical mobility and in terms of his or her emotional and mental mobility. They are indeed interconnected and dependent on each other.

But one cannot be free if he or she has physical restraints and handicaps, and one cannot be free if he or she has emotional or mental restraints or handicaps, either. If we lack freedom, it basically means that our possibilities are limited and that our ability to choose from a wide variety of choices is confined or restrained. If we are dependent on substances like food, alcohol, drugs, and sex, our freedom is also limited.

By answering the calls of the Dark Horse and its desires, we are choosing servitude and slavish dependency. That is the irony of the narcissist, who so much wants to believe he or she is in control.

By choosing to be the center of the universe, humans sacrifice freedom and opt to ride the Dark Horse—straight to the gulag.

CHAPTER 8

THE GLOBAL
COMMUNITY AND
THE DARK HORSE

"*I* see myself as a global citizen" might sound like the words of a modern version of an enlightened person. He or she might see him- or herself as without prejudice, open-minded, easily adaptable, nonjudgmental, unafraid of change, and tolerant of varying values and beliefs.

This person would be extremely conscious of his or her self and the world and environment around him or her, and ever mindful of the fact that all people must coexist in a world of mutual need and interdependence.

The enlightened person of today would be a truly international and progressive being, integrating all of his or her actions and desires into the new matrix of life, commonly referred to as the global community, which is steered by business and politics. In this global community, business and politics—by-products of modernity, a secular society, and the paradigm of the West—have come to dominate our collective consciousness so much so that the world is starting to get its perception of truth and reality exclusively from them.

They have become omnipresent. They are present in all spheres of human activity unlike at any other time in human history. They are present in matters relating to family, education, government, community, health, and even faith.

Having become an ever-present part of our lives, they have also come to appropriate a major portion of our lives. Nowhere is this more evident than in the way the media accords prime space to business and political news and analysis—at the local, state, national, and international levels— with greater emphasis on the global community.

This global community, however, is an artificial construct, designed and created for one specific purpose: to fuel our desires. Everything about this global world is constructed on artificial concepts and perfectly lubricated by high-tech machinery to make it easy for everybody to satisfy his or her body's cravings and material needs.

Almost everything about this global world is designed to create in us artificial desires, transform those wants into needs, and then make it easier for us to acquire them.

This attempt to coordinate our lives so the machinery of commerce can run smoothly has completely reconfigured the many components of the matrix of human life today—so much so that business and politics have reached a dominant level in our consciousness.

As a result most people find themselves more and more connected to and associated with the mind and body and the world of desire and illusion—and more and more connected to fulfilling the objects and beings of our desires, and not the spiritual ones. This mentality, which is an outgrowth of the paradigm of the West, is not only keeping people on the Dark Horse, but it is also making them gallop on it.

This begs the questions: Is a human being a spiritual being, or is he or she a material being? Is a human being a political-business animal, or is he or she a manifestation of the spiritual? Is he or she born into this world to satisfy the senses or to rise above them?

What is humanity's purpose for being? Is it here to promote the interests of the corporate world, the nation states, and the global community, or is it here to promote and express the love and virtues of the spiritual within?

Unfortunately, if you look around the world today, you will see that people have clearly answered that humans are material beings, in which case, they prefer to limit their scope and vision, not widen it.

By associating and identifying with the global community, and the paradigm of the West, humans have chosen to connect to and identify with their little self, or ego, not with their spiritual self.

In our global society today, a world wholly motivated and fueled by the interests of commerce and politics, i.e., the material world, we find ourselves more and more connected to and associated with the body/mind nexus and the world of desire and illusion—the world of the Dark Horse.

Never before in the history of civilization have we been so well informed about things, never before have we had such a heightened awareness of our self, and never before in history have we been so ignorant.

This ignorance comes about primarily because humans have been conditioned by the paradigm of the West—and its artificial, dualistic, and materialistic interpretation of reality—to believe that seeking objects and beings in the external world can bring them happiness.

But it is not making them feel better. For all their education and wealth, global citizens have become dissatisfied and discontented with the nature of things, and they have started to yearn for the things they do not have and to lament about their own nature, which has basically become artificial.

According to the most spiritual traditions, there is no ambiguity or mystery about why we are here: We are here because we *chose* to come here. Due to our inability to go beyond our body/mind attachments and our unwillingness or inability to connect with and unite with the spiritual in our former lives, we planted the seeds for our eventual recall to this world called Earth.

We are (today) what we desired in the past, and since we desired more and more fulfillment in our material existence, we were given this location on Earth, where everything and everybody operates on the material plane.

Unless and until we are able to renounce our desires and the mind's identification with the body and its senses (the Dark Horse), we will forever be doomed to reenact this same drama, time and time again.

According to these spiritual traditions, our coming into existence is no accident. There are no accidents, just previous causes and their effects. If we ever hope to end this cycle of birth, death, and rebirth, we must come to eliminate the cause of our existence here on Earth, which is ignorance and the illusion it creates: that all things are permanent.

The nearer we get to our spirit (not the ego/self), the nearer we get to selflessness. Conversely, the nearer we get to the ego/self (not the spirit), the nearer we get to selfishness.

By taking the journey inward, we come closer to the self and the world of spirit. By going outward and identifying with material phenomena, like the paradigm of the West and the global community, we get closer to the self and the material world.

The more we come to know and experience the self—our spiritual selves—the more we will come to know and experience love. Similarly, the less we come to know and experience the self, the less we will come to know and experience love, and the more we will experience selfishness. Self-realization is not going to come to us by wearing the newest trends in designer clothes and shoes or using the latest technological advances in communication. But it will come to us when we discover our true nature within and naturally manifest it from without.

At that point, one experiences a perfect and natural balance of energy, where the distribution of what flows in is commensurate to and perfectly matched by that which flows out. When that happens, when one reaches a state of perfect balance and harmony, the center of gravity shifts from the center out—or from the source within us to those who are in need of its vibration outside—to the family, the community, the nation, the world, and the universe.

When one reaches this state, there is no limit to the amount of love one expresses, nor is there a way one can confine or contain it to individuals, groups, or borders. Giving love and feeling compassion are natural expressions, just as light is the natural expression of the sun. The more conscious one becomes of this spiritual (self) reality, the more imperative it is to lead a life whereby only such feelings and activities are present and can manifest. This builds suitable habits and character, and a destiny that matches both.

The divine/Tao is eternal, unchanging, and intransient. This reality can never be perceived at a physical or intellectual level. It surely will not be realized while we are shopping at a mall or while we are online. It is a reality that can only be appreciated at the highest level of spiritual awareness, which can only be attained by going inward. In the vision of the great spiritual traditions that had spirit knowledge and were one with the divine/Tao, no changes whatsoever take place. Who among us today can understand this? In a world not only typified by great change, and driven and fueled by it as well, who would believe that there is such a state where no change exists? The global community we live in today is a world of constant and never-ceasing change and stimulation. Our bodies and senses are literally bombarded and inundated by all manners of stimuli, and our minds are forever reacting to, analyzing, and disseminating all the varied information we receive every second of the day.

Adapting to this change is the only way we know of surviving it. How could we find a world in which change does not exist? It would have to be death itself. This has come to represent the greatest fear of the so-called global denizens: a world without change, a lifeless state, a world where our minds and bodies would cease to exist anymore.

Yet, if there is anyone among us who actually believes there is a state of existence higher than the one we are living in and who wishes to explore the possibility of attaining such a level of spirituality, the first thing he or she would have to do is to shut out all the stimuli, disconnect with the outside world, and turn the attention inward.

He or she would have to turn off or shut down the computer, television, cell phone, iPod, and all the artificial components that make up the global community and are the main source of our spiritual blindness. Only then, when he or she has tuned out and tuned in, can one begin to discover the spiritual world.

In materialistic terms, biologists would say that everybody alive, indeed everything alive, owes its existence to its biochemical components and how they are ordered and contained in the DNA matrix. But this is a limited way of looking at reality, by confining the scope of analysis to the material world of phenomena only.

If these scientists would also turn their gaze and analysis inward, something they have rarely done, they would see the whole matrix of life, including the cosmos and even DNA. They would see, as others did before them, that infinity itself lies within us—not in the structures of DNA but in the eternity and changeless reality of the divine/Tao—and it is there to see, inside and within our intrinsic nature.

The advocates of a global community, however, are not concerned about marketing or promoting this kind of spiritual self; rather they are concerned with and focused on guiding people to identify with the material self and to regress to lower levels of consciousness, such as consumption and the bottom line.

Like a funeral home that thrives on death, global marketers thrive on ignorance and the presence of a thriving community of pleasure seekers and fantasy seekers. After all, those who are interested in and connected to the Tao and the spirit world would hardly be interested in connecting to or using artificial devices or shopping at artificially constructed markets.

The global marketers profit from humanity's distance from the Tao/ God, not its proximity, in the same way that pharmaceutical companies and the medical establishment profit from humans' illnesses and not their good health. In both cases, there is hardly any motivation to see that people are living happy, healthy, and spiritually fulfilled lives.

In a spiritual state, the mind will be elevated and calm, providing us with good health, peace, and longevity. Shouldn't that also be the goal of each and every one of us today? Unfortunately, we will not find these qualities in the marketplace; nor are corporations and governments looking to satisfy those needs in us.

Instead, we are looking for eternal joy and happiness, and the global community satisfies this misguided search by offering a plethora of products that can turn us into emotional and sensory junkies and delude us into thinking they will give us permanent joy and bliss. But such worldly pursuits as joy and bliss and the pleasures they bring to our worldly arena are neither pure nor permanent—nor is it healthy to pursue them. If a thing is capable of giving us pleasure, it is also capable of giving us pain.

Pleasure and pain go together because things in nature always reverse at some stage, and pleasure and joy are no exceptions. Pleasure gives birth to pain, and joy is the nursery of suffering. By seeking pleasure and joy, we have already planted the seeds for pain.

How does one recognize global consciousness? Global consciousness comes about with a cultivation of attachment, a state of extreme passion, individuality, and desire. One's focus is on outward appearances and values, largely and predominantly artificial. The center of gravity begins with the self and seeks union with other selves of like mind and mentality.

The purpose of one's life is to be in control, i.e., to be the center of the universe. One is obsessed with time and space, and racing feverishly against the effects that the passage of time and space have on one's age, beauty, sex, wealth, status, power, and fame.

How does one recognize spirituality? It comes about with the cultivation of detachment, a state of extreme and supreme dispassion. In this state, one no longer cares about or identifies with those aspects of the body-mind matrix. As an extension, one distances him- or herself from the global community and its acquisitive, destructive mentality.

At this point, as one turns his or her back on the paradigm of the West and this global network, he or she goes deeper and deeper into a higher state of spiritual existence. All components of the life matrix associated by those participants of the global community become part of nonreality, and they cease to exist for him or her.

There is no *I*, no *you*, no *right*, no *wrong*. There is nothing to advocate or any special interests to promote. There are no flags to die for and no weapons to kill with. There are no more fears, nor anything to worry over or obsess about. There remains only one reality: the world of spirit; all else remains meaningless.

And here is the secret of living. When one realizes that the mind-body is only a vehicle to function on this earth then one's life mission comes to manifest not in terms of a body consciousness but in terms of a spiritual consciousness- and in fulfilling the needs of the spirit and not those of the body and mind.

One should cringe at the thought that so many people embrace this global community because it means they are identifying reality not with the spirit or Tao, but with the ego and the material world.

But that is precisely what the paradigm of the West and the global way does to us. It stimulates all our senses, and it activates and brings out all our illusions and desires. In doing so, it encourages us to identify with the ego and the Dark Horse, and not with the spiritual side of the soul.

CHAPTER 9

LOOKING TO THE SKY

*W*hen humans began their search, they looked outside of their bodies and outside of their awareness. They were looking up and away from their bodies and imagining a truth that somehow was to be found beyond their personal capacity to perceive it. Mostly they looked up to the sky to seek these answers.

But the responses they got from looking to the sky have not always been the same; in fact, they have usually been greeted by two different and contrary responses. One group has felt a sense of fear, coupled with awe and reverence; the other group has felt a sense of wonder and adventure, with a desire to find out what lurks behind all the darkness, if anything at all.

From the first response was born a belief that there was a hidden, mysterious, and all-powerful force behind it all, a creator of everything. From the second response was born a conviction that there was a material and explainable force behind it all.

The first response eventually went on to create religion, and the second response ultimately went on to form the basis of science. Together they would form the paradigm of the West. In the process, humans came to identify only two ways of finding the truth: by hearsay, i.e., from the words and experiences of others, or by experiencing it directly, i.e., going there personally and finding out what was there.

One group was willing to believe in and trust the words of others, others who had come down from the sky to tell them about it. The other group was not; those in that group had to see for themselves.

One group of people was content remaining where they were and studying previously held truths or previously reported truths. The other group of people was not; they had to go outside to find the truth, to experience it directly. They had to see and learn for themselves.

One group feared change and grasped at what was known; the other group embraced change and set out to redefine reality. One group became the preserver of tradition and crafted rituals and dogma to formalize its accepted versions of truth. These people became the ministers of truth. Members of the other group became the explorers setting out in unchartered territory and unknown frontiers to discover the truth. They became the pioneers of truth.

But it hasn't always been this way, seeing truth in dualistic terms. Before the arrival of organized religions, Western science, and the paradigm of the West, these two divergent perspectives were able to coexist harmoniously. They were not viewed so much in opposition to each other as they were seen as complements to each other, i.e., the Eros and Logos of the human predicament, or the energetic forces of yin and yang, matter and energy.

The key was to find a balance between them, not to make a choice between them, and not to judge one as superior to the other, but to get them both to work properly—relative to time and space, and relative to the human frame and condition. With the arrival of organized religion, whose believers had clearly looked up at the sky and felt fear, absolutism was born and humans were coerced to make a choice.

Humans were forced to go outside their bodies and look beyond their self for answers; they were forced to look where their senses could never go and where their intellect was not permitted to enter. They were forced to believe in something they had never seen, heard, or touched, and to believe in something that was totally irrational and required a leap of faith to accept.

It may have been irrational for humans to surrender like that, thinking there was something other than them to guide and protect themselves, and something greater than them to live for. But they did it anyway because doing so gave them a greater sense of peace and serenity—not to mention, a feeling of safety and protection.

Humans believed, despite their doubts. In so doing, they surrendered to a greater force, and in return they knew where they belonged in the grand scheme of things. There was no need to question it anymore; they had faith, and that faith made them feel so secure and so protected.

For a thousand years, one group of people lived this way, unquestioning their existence. They didn't look up to the sky, asking who they were and why they were here. They knew the answer; there was no need to look anymore. They were God's children, serving the Divine. That was all; that was enough.

There was order in life—a purpose, a structure, a hierarchy—and people adapted to these external forces and controls with quiet resignation. They were part of a greater community, a fellowship, with like-minded spirits. They didn't question anything anymore, and they didn't feel any need to, either. They belonged.

But that peace and stability, that unity of purpose and identity, that feeling of having a well-ordered and defined place in the world could not last forever because it came at the expense of the other group—the inquiring, inquisitive, intellectual, and adventurous individuals who refused to accept things the way they were told. There had to be a reason for the way things were, and they meant to find out what it was, despite all the opposition and obstacles organized religion put in their way.

Similarly, they looked up to the sky, but they did not see what the religionists saw—some irrational and paternal-like force looking down on them and controlling them like pawns on a chessboard, moving them hither and yon at its whim and fancy. They saw numbers, forms, and patterns—and the world has never been the same since.

Until about five hundred years ago, until the time of Galileo, most people's search led them to believe, or at least not to deny, in a divine being. But things started to change dramatically with the arrival of science. Brick by brick, the edifice upon which religion was constructed—and the core of humans' meaning in life—started to unravel.

By the nineteenth century, the gloves came off, and scientists started to openly challenge religion's supremacy by calling it an "opiate to society."

Some even dared to openly say that God was dead. After a century of wars and hundreds of millions killed, it was hard to find volunteers to argue to the contrary.

Emboldened by their advances, science urged people to see religion for what it really was: an illusion and nothing more. The scientists said that God was only a symbol of an infantile desire for a father (or mother) and that it was time to grow up. The truth had come out: The awe and reverence that people once felt for God was only a narcissistic fantasy!

Science had good reason to feel confident. Scientists had delivered on their promises; religion had not. People were better off because of what they had *done*, not because of what religion had *said*. The proof was in the pudding: religion was all about words; science was about deeds. After all, hadn't they made the world a better place?

Unquestionably, people's material well-being had improved dramatically on all accounts, and they had science to thank for it. It had taken them out of the forests and clothed them; it had taken them out of the deserts and educated them; it had taken women off the fields and put them in offices.

There was not a man or woman alive who had not been touched or improved by the vast tentacles of science. It had liberated countries, women, and slaves; it had eliminated castes and segregation; it had built the foundation for eliminating poverty and illiteracy; and it had virtually modernized every institution on earth from economics and politics to medicine and psychology.

Religion had never been able to deliver like that. It had people living in the past by worshipping dead people; science got them to live in the future by building the foundation to succeed.

Religion got people to live in ignorance; science gave them an education and turned them into millionaires. How could one argue against their successes? Science literally had taken people out of darkness and had given them light. Not even God had been able to do that!

And science had done it all without divine intervention or grace. It had done it all on its own merits, with its own blood, sweat, and tears, and based on the intelligence and skill of the people, not on some unknown, unseen, and outside divine intelligence. Science did it with mere mortals, right here on Earth, in the Kingdom of Man. What did religion have to show for itself? What material contributions had it ever made to humankind?

When humans were ignorant, religion could speak to them about their gods and saints and the miracles they had performed, and they were easily influenced. But it was child's play compared to the kind of feats science is able to perform today. There is little that science cannot do; it can just about create—and destroy—anything. It can give life, any form of life, and then take it away. Science has become our omnipresent and omnipotent creator on Earth because it is able to do what we thought only God could do. Who needs God anymore when we have science? And we don't even have to pray to it either, or have blind faith in it. We can see it, hear it, and touch it, and it's right there at our fingertips to use whenever we need or desire it.

What good has religion done in comparison? Has it done anything to improve people's health, wealth, or longevity, or even their day-to-day existence? Just go to where science is not evident, where people still live in ignorance but are still devout believers, and look at their conditions. Little has changed for them in all their years of faith. They are still materially poor, uneducated servants to the rich, and they are dying at young ages.

Now, after several thousand years of faith and devotion, God's omnipresence and omnipotence have come under question, since the creations of humanity have proved to be more powerful and successful than God's.

People are everywhere, controlling everything, even destroying everything, and God has never tried to stop them. Why not if He is so powerful? What good has God done to stop them? In fact, what good has He ever done?

CHAPTER 10

MODERN MAN

*M*odern men and women are very lost and very confused—they just don't know it. In the past they knew it. It was called despair, and it came on when they looked up to the sky with bemusement and got no response. All their questions about who they were, why they were here, and what the meaning of the life was went answered.

The silence was deafening, but it spoke volumes. Humans were nothing but specks of dust with no meaning or purpose in an impersonal and mechanistic world, with nobody or nothing to protect them or care about them, either.

They were all alone in the world. There was no rhyme or reason for their existence on Earth and no hope for their existence after their stay on Earth, either. Human life had no more meaning than an inconsequential snail or molecule. It was an intolerable realization. Even worse, there was no cure for this malaise, just jumping headfirst into the abyss.

It was called a crisis of existence, and paradoxically, the only way of exiting from the despair was by surrendering to it. Basically, it came about because people didn't know what to believe anymore; they were hopelessly divided between science and religion, and mind and body.

On the one side was religion, and on the other side was science, both forever identifying, interpreting, and classifying truth. One group of people continued reading very, very old texts to define the outer horizons, insisting they were *speaking* the truth; the other group kept making bigger and more expensive instruments to take us to the outer limits, insisting they were *showing* us the truth.

Caught in the middle of this seemingly eternal fight for supremacy were the people, powerless to do anything about it—indeed, powerless to act at all. Every aspect of their life had been classified and labeled. Regardless of what they touched, smelled, saw, heard, or thought, it had already been identified by others, critiqued by others, and differentiated by others.

What was the point of life in this state? The people had received no answers to their previous questions, so in despair they threw their hands up to the sky in contempt and fell deeper and deeper into a big black hole. This was a crisis brought on by an industrial revolution and the analytical human mind and its queries of who they were and where they fit in the grand scheme of things, and the silence that followed.

Things are very different today. Now after years and years of going everywhere to see the sky, and after investigating every word ever written about what came down from the sky, modern men and women know everything and anything about the sky and have critiqued every syllable spoken about it. So what's the point of asking?

Nowadays there is little mystery in life. How could there be when everything has already been discovered? Besides outer space, what is to be explored? What great mystery is to be unraveled? Breaking a genetic code, discovering a new chemical compound? People nowadays find more solace in Marvel comics than they do in looking to the sky or in reading scriptures.

Modern men and women do not look up to the sky the way people in the past did; even if they do, they will never look to the sky the way those in the past did—with a sense of awe and wonder. Awe and wonder come from a sense of humility and respect, but such qualities were lost long ago when mystery was taken away from life.

What is there to feel awe about? Wonder? People today have already been told what is out there, what it's made of, how and when it began, and the laws behind the whole universe. They only need ask NASA, so what's the point of looking there ourselves?

In addition life is no longer an adventure to personally experience, a way to create and form an identity of our own regardless of how small or insignificant. People today are not following the stars—or their own stars, for that matter—to find the answers. They do not look to heaven; nor do they feel a link to it.

In the past, it didn't matter how large or small your imprint was; the emphasis was on quality not quantity. What mattered was that it was your mark and nobody else's. It was your imprint, and the way you lived life identified the kind of mark you left behind. You could see it "written" on your face.

It was your own signature; you carved yourself. You were the artist and the art; you were one and the same. Hadn't God done the same thing when He created the universe? You were unique. Suffering was not to be avoided; it was to be embraced. That was how God was made manifest—through the journey of the soul and all one's travails in life.

But in order to do that, one had to ask questions and seek out the answers from above and from within. Your voice was your master. "Know thyself" was the catchword, and living in nature and being one with nature was the way. It was about uniting not dividing; one knew he or she had arrived when word and deed became one, and the measure of a person was in how integrated he or she was. For only in balance and unity could the "real" person emerge.

But that was before; it isn't that way now. There hasn't been such a concept of balance and unity around for a very long time, not since the Cartesian Compromise came about in the seventeenth century. At that time, when it was agreed that the mind and body were separate entities, science and religion went their separate ways, taking with them body and mind respectively and any sense of balance and unity.

Nowadays the modern man and woman rarely consider their nature or essence; indeed, they no longer consider nature at all. People are much more comfortable living in the city than in the countryside. As a result, they have few opportunities to experience nature and its ways. If people have any contact with nature at all, apart from being tourists, it may only be from going to a park for a walk or peeping out the window to steal a glimpse of the sun setting.

Instead, all they experience is artificial living at every level and all times of the day and night. The five faculties or senses, which were once used for inventing tools or examining life, are now used almost exclusively for indulging in artificial things. The things that people touch, smell, taste, hear, and see are mostly artificial, and if any are natural, few people can afford to buy them.

If one were to observe an individual on a normal twenty-four-hour day, in an average city, one would be hard-pressed to find that person making contact with anything that is natural at all. Such is the world for the average individual living in the city and suburbs nowadays—his or her whole world and all his or her senses are completely dominated by artificial things. Even the air that we breathe and the water that we drink are primarily artificial.

Incredibly, entire populations of modern people around the world have never tasted a drop of fresh spring water; nor have they ever washed their clothes in natural water. Generations of modern people have never put their hands in the soil, and they have never eaten anything without chemical additives, preservatives, and hormones; nor have they ever smelled anything without artificial aromas.

Nowadays, little that modern men and women do in their daily affairs has anything to do with nature at all. They eat food made from chemicals, modified genes, and hormones, and they can eat them at any time of the year in any place of the world. They go to work in a mechanized vehicle and work inside an artificial building with artificial lights and artificial air.

They use electronic machines to connect with people and the world around them. They wash and dry clothes in electronic appliances and prepare food in radioactive and electronic appliances. They heat and cool their dwellings with central air, they get information from electronic machines, and they receive health cures from high-tech equipment and chemicals.

They get their knowledge while passively sitting in a chair and listening to lectures; listening to news; listening to professors, priests, and gurus; reading books; watching TV; or looking at electronic windows, computer screens, or mobile phones.

They receive little knowledge from directly experiencing the nature around them, and they learn about their gods from a book or from the interpreters of a book, not from the spirits/gods communicating with them directly through the elements, up in the mountains.

They get pleasure from artificial stimulants and artificially flavored food, artificially sounding music, artificially painted and moving pictures, artificially contrived and man-made diversions, and artificially stimulated sexual pleasure and contact; not from natural foods, flavors, beauty, sounds, and sites, and natural stimulation from the flowers blooming in spring, snows blanketing the trees in winter, and the warmth of companionship in harmony with the natural cycles of life.

They get their sense of purpose from personal ambition, a competitive spirit, and their ability to realize their own dreams and aspirations—separate from and in opposition to their fellow humans—not from cultivating their virtues and living in cooperation and in spiritual harmony with others, at one with all and at one with the universe.

And they get value of life from satisfying the needs and desires of their senses and aggrandizing their ego—the Dark Horse—not by overcoming them.

Almost everything about modern life as we know it in modern times is virtually programmed and conditioned by man-made (artificial) values and things—food, knowledge, connections, politics, commerce, education, pleasure, information, stimulants, and beauty.

Even love is artificially contrived in that modern life has taken one of humankind's most natural instincts—to give love—and transformed it into something that must be accompanied by an idealized emotion, not just a reaction to a natural instinct, and something modern people must acquire. Now it's all about *getting* love.

More than anything else, modern men and women consider themselves outside the reach of nature and, as a result, outside its natural laws and patterns. This has led modern people to behave, consciously and unconsciously, as though they are no longer a part of nature.

In the human world, there is no concept of holism and balancing the inner and outer worlds, not since it was decided that only the quantifiable aspects of matter are real and the immaterial world was discarded as irrelevant and unreal.

Humans are here to be members of the global community, to satisfy the body, to overindulge in the senses, and to titillate the mind. And they get all the encouragement and support they need from a modern, materialistic, scientific, and secular world, which does everything to capitalize on their ignorance, foment their illusions, and fuel their cravings.

If people today look anywhere for answers, they look to the bank, to the government, to the department stores, to the websites, to the politicians, to the doctors, to the scientists, to the bookshops, to the stockbrokers, to the accountants, to the celebrities, to the talk show hosts, to the iPods, and to the Internet search engines. They look everywhere but inside. And they don't integrate; they separate and divide.

In this world, what is the point of revealing a soul? Besides, what is the soul anyway, and where is it? And what does God have to do with the neutral and impersonal forces of evolution, physics, electromagnetic fields, megabytes, quantum mechanics, DNA, Western medicine, and shopping centers? In fact, where does He fit in the cosmic drama? He seems so … irrelevant. In fact, some might argue that the big question in life is no longer what *our* place in the universe is, but what *God's* place is.

Besides, what good ever came from thinking about why you are here and wringing your hands in despair? Indeed, not since mind and body went their separate ways—and wisdom was jettisoned from human reality in the name of knowledge—have people made much of a to-do about knowing themselves and the whys and wherefores in this life.

This is a new period, a new age, punctuated by activity, individuality, and fulfilling one's dreams and ambitions. In this world there is little time for self-reflection and contemplation; it is time to get on with life, to be practical, and to stop thinking.

What is the point of asking all the questions anyway since nobody could ever answer them? Be practical, be positive, be grateful, and above all else, be happy. Be like the Americans—and just do it!

Despite this positive spin and despite increased wealth and well-being, modern men and women are feeling neither happy nor grateful. Instead they are feeling consumed by fear and loneliness and a terrifying realization that this might be as good as it gets, and that is clearly a depressing thought!

How could this be? People today have everything, and still it is not enough? They are feeling sicker and more depressed. Why? How? It's unthinkable and—to many who are poor and do without—unimaginable. Why are modern men and women so unhappy and so unwell? Who knows?

They are wealthy, educated, and free; they are born and bred in a secular society and know little if anything about life and almost nothing about their self. All their exploring outside and beyond the body has not rendered any great or irrevocable truths. They are still just guessing or repeating age-old tales and are none the wiser for it.

Is it any wonder why Westerners today don't ask many questions anymore? Besides, they know their truth; they know their reality. They are here to pay taxes and to die—those are the certainties they live by, and there is no point in asking much or looking to the sky for answers. Neither can change their reality. But it's so depressing.

So in their depression, people today just give up trying. They give up asking, and they give up wondering. They take meds instead; that way they can't think, that way they can't feel, and that way they can't hear the truth. But at least that way they can make it through another day—and that makes them happy.

And in this state, when they are mindless and taking antidepressants, they do not know that they are lost and confused. Thank God for that!

CHAPTER 11

THE ABSURDITY
OF HAPPINESS

*F*or the ancients, nature was the key to happiness. By living in nature, one observes the patterns and sees the nature, or essence, of things. In the same way, humans are manifesting their nature by observing and understanding the patterns outside and inside, above and below, materially and immaterially. By doing so, they are expressing their divine nature, or essence. In fact, there is no difference.

For the ancients, life without nature is no life at all, and the human being is not a human living outside of it. As people unite their nature with nature—their essence with the essence of nature—they are also uniting the essence of the divine/Tao with their own divine/spiritual essence. That is their goal in life and the reason for being.

By uniting human existence in life with the human's goal in life, he or she is living a good life, and that good life will bring him or her happiness. Seen in this way, happiness is not an emotion like joy or a state of being.

Happiness does not come about as a result of fulfilling one's dreams or ambitions; nor does it come about by satisfying one's desires or by possessing an object or person. These are ephemeral, certain not to last. Happiness is an activity, not an entity. It is characteristic of a good life, that is, a life in which a person fulfills his or her (intrinsic) nature in a virtuous, balanced, and natural way.

For the ancients, all life occurs within the circle of nature, meaning all things are connected and mutually dependent on each other. When the elements of nature are in balance, life is harmonic and flourishes. When the balance of forces is upset, disaster comes. Humans represent the juncture between heaven and earth and are, therefore, greatly influenced by both. Sustained and kept alive by both, humans are incapable of separating from either, but when they try, disaster comes.

Within this reality, the world is seen holistically with each and every aspect of nature connected and linked to another, and life is about dynamic, constantly shifting relationships of one functional system with another, always within the context of the whole. No aspects of nature are fixed and permanent; nor are they independent and discrete entities.

By the same token, no aspects of a human personality are fixed and permanent, nor can one life function as independent and separate from another. Our thoughts create our emotions, our emotions shape our body, our body affects our spirit, our spirit affects our mind, and our lives affect others' lives.

So, for the ancients, if one wants to live a happy and fulfilling life, one has to start by living in nature and by living life naturally, which one does by balancing his or her internal world with his or her external world. This comes about when one is able to successfully balance the forces of nature from above (heaven) with the forces of nature below (Earth) within his or her own body and mind.

Thus, balance and harmony, as well as good health and wellness, can only come about when people follow the balancing principles of the universe in everyday living—not only in the intellect or theory, but also in nature. In this way, living in harmony with one's internal and external environments—knowledge and wisdom, reason and emotion, material and immaterial—becomes the ultimate goal of life.

For thousands of years, life was seen in this holistic way. So if people wanted to be happy, they had to balance, not eliminate, these opposing forces beginning with their self. In other words, if they wanted to be happy, they had to take care of their needs both on a mundane level (body and mind) and on a supramundane level (spirit and soul). In this way, they were uniting their heavenly nature and needs with their earthly needs and nature. And they did this by being both in nature and of nature.

On the other hand, unhappiness comes about because there is a disturbance in our inner world, which occurs because we have severed the material world from the immaterial world. When this happens, humans no longer see a link to heaven above and instead preoccupy and identify their self with their materialistic, physical, and earthly needs. Life then becomes "spirit-less" and "soul-less," and being here on Earth loses any meaning and purpose, save their never-ending desires and preoccupation with their realization.

So if we want to be happy, according to the ancients, we have to rediscover our true nature and origins. To do that we have to awaken the spirit; this, in turn, will help the soul overcome its desires (the desires of the Dark Horse) on earth and reunite with heaven.

With this goal in mind, the ancients articulated a way of living life designed in such a way as to foster balance and harmony—among opposing forces—within a whole, integrated system of life and living. Thus in balance, people will find their connections again, and once they do, they will also find a unity of purpose and existence; good health, happiness, and well-being will naturally follow.

Enter the paradigm of the West, which does not promote a philosophy of balance and harmony. Instead it proclaims a war on nature as the chief cause of human suffering. It does not see nature as a benevolent—or for that matter, meaningful—force that people have to unite with to find their purpose. It does not see humans' essence as manifesting in nature or through it, either. Indeed, it doesn't even recognize an essence in humans at all! Nature is not divine; it is an uncertain, chaotic, and unpredictable force—and the primary source and origin of all human problems.

As a result, the central quest of the paradigm of the West is to gain dominance and dominion over nature by conquering and controlling it or, at the very least, harnessing its powers for profit and keeping its power at bay from humanity.

Over time, the paradigm of the West would eventually come to dominate Westerners' thinking, so much so that over time any consideration of people's inner world—the world of wisdom and spirituality, and the world of nature and our own inner nature—would lose all relevance in terms of our happiness. Only the external world and the world of matter would be considered.

Instead the (Western) world would come to see humans, systems, or governments as separate from nature and something that could be taken apart and reduced to parts like a machine. In this way of seeing reality, all people are alike, all problems or disease come from the same cause, and all treatment is the same for people, systems, and governments.

This conceptual model excludes that nature, and the total condition of a person, a system, or a government seriously affects one's susceptibility to disease or happiness. One must find a singular and material cause and then destroy or seek it respectively. That's the central quest: total annihilation of nature, both internally and externally. Thus, the universe does not express a purpose anymore; it is simply governed by impersonal physical laws independent of how we hope to fit in the grand scheme of things. The universe is just a vast, cold, inhuman, indifferent, and mechanical entity. The best we can hope from this kind of meaningless and impersonal existence is to investigate the laws behind this machine and see how it works.

Because of this view, nature is no longer perceived as the book written by God or as a visible expression of the divine/Tao, in which humans find their meaning in life by participating in and becoming one with nature. It does not have an essence, and there is no goal for the sake of which a thing is the way it is. Nature is just impersonal stuff that we can know only when we separate from it and put it under a microscope.

Now, after three centuries of implacable determination to know the real nature of the universe—at the expense of humans' esoteric, unreal, subjective, and unreliable nature – modern men and women are starting to feel the dangerous and debilitating side effects of separating from nature and failing to address our meaning and purpose in life and what can make us happy, if anything.

Modern-day people are really, really unhappy. And though many can express hypotheses about why we are so unhappy (not having a meaning and purpose in life is tops on the list), few can offer a cure. It seems almost axiomatic to say, "I have everything I want and need in life, but what's the point?"

We have the things to make us happy, we have the money to make us happy, we have the education to make us happy, and we have the free and democratic government to make us happy, but still happiness eludes us. Why?

It seems that contemporary people's pursuit of knowledge has also brought about a complementary pursuit: the pursuit of happiness. Unfortunately, each of us is pursuing his or her own goals independent of the other. Instead of uniting the two, knowledge and happiness, as the ancients advised, they are irreconcilably separated, even at odds with one another.

In fact, the knowledge seekers might argue that the pursuit of happiness is the cause of unhappiness, since it depends on sentiments and feelings, which are unpredictable, irrational, unreliable, and temporary. The happiness seekers might counter by arguing that the pursuit of knowledge has led to humanity's loss of innocence and its divinity and the main reason everybody feels so hopelessly unhappy in the first place.

Sad truth be known, happiness in today's world has become an absurdity. It is impossible to define, impossible to pursue, impossible to measure, and even impossible to talk about in an intelligent way. Indeed, many argue that pursuing it will bring about the opposite effect; paradoxically, not pursuing it will bring about feelings of emptiness, isolation, and even depression.

In some circles the word *happiness* is not used any longer. *Wellness* has replaced the word happiness. In other circles, people say that happiness cannot come to those who are aware of it, or if you are aware of it, you can't be happy.

The absurdity of happiness does not stop there, either. There are a whole host of ideas about happiness, such as happiness is not a permanent state but a temporary state, happiness is a cycle of exhaustion and renewal, and happiness is more like a range, with contentment at the bottom and exaltation at the top.

Happiness is not a state but a process; happiness is never the same for two people; happiness is not attainable, but tranquility or contentment are; happiness can only come by treating something else; and happiness is subjective, a subjective well-being, or SWB.

In fact, if one scours the landscape of the world looking for a definition of happiness and looks beyond interpreting it in relative terms, one will witness, by and large, an unspoken admission that the human being is basically a fallen creature that can never attain happiness.

But if happiness is not possible, what is but the illusion of happiness! Happiness may not be attainable, but few people in the world today question the surrogates of happiness and the demonstrable effects they can have on everybody.

So instead of pursuing happiness in the classic sense, contemporary people have turned to pursuing the artificial and materialistic accouterments of happiness, such as fame, money, success, power, sex, affluence, pleasure, family, fun, and joy. In these areas people are not so ambivalent or pessimistic; instead they pursue them with reckless abandon.

Can you blame them? After all, what is the alternative? To say that we are here for no reason at all? To admit that our lives here on Earth have no meaning or purpose whatsoever and that happiness is just an illusion, to surrender to the hard facts of scientific and materialistic reality? Happiness may not be real, but who cares? Movies are not real either, but we love watching them.

Reality depresses me; illusion makes me feel better. My home life depresses me, so I will watch the idyllic homes of others. My work life depresses me, so I will escape by viewing the successful or unsuccessful careers of others. My beauty long ago abandoned me, so I will fantasize about entering a world where nobody ages and I am still attractive and seductive. My God never hears my cries, so I will ride into space and look for Him there in the form of aliens.

Modern men and women may be living a great fallacy, believing that they can possess anything they want, and believing the illusion that fulfillment is not only possible but easy and inevitable. They may even have swallowed the marketing gimmicks and illusions propagated by big business and advertising companies, along with the propaganda and lie advanced by governments and educational institutions.

But what is the alternative?

That we are all here for no meaning at all, that there is no such thing as happiness, no good life and no purpose, no greater significance on this planet than anything else, not even a mosquito? Who can deal with that? Bring on the celebrities, bring on the flags, bring on the wars, bring on the religions, bring on the guns, bring on the cars, bring on the sex, bring on the violence, bring on the alcohol, bring on the drugs, bring on the family, and bring on the world of illusion!

Modern people may have become happy fantasists living in the world of fantasy, dreams, and virtual realities, but is there any other option, considering the other possibility?

If humans are fallen creatures, all alone and bereft of divine protection, connection, and unity, what is the point in doing anything, save escaping from this depressing reality? Is it any wonder that so many people are online, taking antidepressants, returning to religious fundamentalism, masturbating to web porn, and blowing people away indiscriminately?

In this artificial world—in which humanity has no natural ties, physically or spiritually, to heaven and nature anymore and where humans are under siege from terrorists and runaway viruses—people have little choice but to stick with artifice; the alternative is just too threatening. In the other world, the so-called natural world, they would feel too defenseless, too powerless, and too vulnerable.

Better to stick to the artificial world, where people feel—have the illusion—that they are in control. Such is the primary condition for living and surviving in our world today.

CHAPTER 12

GONE ARE THE DAYS ...

*H*onor comes to those who have a clear sense of personal dignity and a widespread, not narrow, interpretation of self-respect. To possess such self-respect, one must be in possession of good character; to be in possession of good character, one must be in possession of virtue. To be in possession of virtue, one must also have an unusual sense of shame. Without shame there can be no real virtues, no real morals, no real manner, and no real sense of self. And without shame there can be no real honor, as there is nothing so credible to back up one's honor.

Dishonor is the payback to those who have lost their reputation, to those who have stained their name and family, and to those who have lost their character and integrity. Shame is what is felt as a consequence of losing one's honor because by losing one's honor, one also loses his or her self and link to the divine.

This is why one must always be on guard for the ways of the Dark Horse because it can make us succumb to our desires and, in the process, bring dishonor and shame into our lives. The Dark Horse is not concerned with righteousness and honor; it is concerned with greed and desire. The Dark Horse is part of the soul, but it leads us away from our divine origins and takes us to the sensory world and the world of mortals. The Dark Horse is part of the soul, but it is the negative—or dark—side of the soul.

All souls are immortal, with or without the Dark Horse. But not all souls are divine; one must possess virtue—in particular, righteousness—to be divine. And to do that, one must follow the ways of heaven and earth.

When the ancients admonished the people to follow heaven and earth, they were admonishing the people to follow the *ways* of heaven and earth. For it is in the ways of heaven and earth that people can observe true love, unconditional and without preconception and judgment. Heaven and earth give equally; heaven loves me and others equally.

The ancients admonished the people to make heaven the object of life, and make awe and reverence for heaven the mission in life. They did not discuss the nature of personal love as in our age; instead the ancients asked the people to make heaven their partner. By making heaven one's partner in life, one always attempts to personify heavenly qualities and one can only do that by bringing out his or her intrinsic nature.

For the ancients, the primary goal in life was building character; intelligence and knowledge were secondary. The three principal goals to achieve in building character are: one, wisdom; two, love; and three, courage. They all derive from one's intrinsic nature. It is not the dogma, morals, or creed that saves a person, but the person who saves him- or herself by building character.

By building character, people have no use for external and artificial aids; they will exemplify them naturally and manifest them when appropriate. Their ambition is not for the gains they get from others' misfortunes, or in acquiring material riches, but in doing the right and honorable thing. One would never sacrifice his conscience for the convenience, utility, or profit of the moment.

Money and how to obtain it was never raised to the level of a virtue as it has become in our times,. Now money is considered the root of all good, the means to justify the ends, while greed is encouraged to keep the economy healthy and keep abundance in our homes, our lifestyle, and our sense of self-worth.

For the ancients, one would choose character to learn, not intelligence; one would choose to cultivate the soul, not fill the head or the bank accounts. The realization of the soul makes the person, not money, not fame, not status, not power, and not the accumulation of knowledge and wealth, but the cultivation of the soul.

Thus true honor lies in fulfilling heaven's decree, and the only way of doing that is by curbing the desires of the Dark Horse and cultivating humanity's intrinsic nature. To do otherwise would bring great dishonor.

Sadly, with the arrival and expansion of the paradigm of the West, the world has witnessed an incredible rise in superficiality and artificiality. No longer are people concerned with building character and acquiring wisdom. Instead people nowadays focus on the acquisition of knowledge, information (knowledge is power), individual rights, power, recognition, wealth, and unlicensed freedom.

Gone are the days of honor and pursuing the virtues of righteousness, principles, sincerity, goodness, and unconditional love and following the ways of heaven. Gone are the days of considering the soul; indeed, gone are the days of allowing people their intrinsic nature, their humaneness, their virtue, their goodness, and their heavenly spirit.

Instead, people are content to follow the ways of Hollywood actors, businessmen, politicians, and priests, and to pursue reality as defined by the paradigm of the West and the Dark Horse that is pulling it along.

CONCLUSION

Nature continuously undergoes the cycle of creation and destruction, and humans are no exception. Indeed, the ability to create and destroy defines the essence of nature; birth is the beginning of death, and death is the beginning of birth. Everything is forever undergoing a reversal and eventual transformation.

—Lama Nicholas

CONCLUSION

Most spiritual traditions believe that the purpose of life is to unfold one's true nature, or soul. To unfold one's true nature is to synchronize one's inner nature with one's external nature, in other words, to reach a perfect harmony between the nature within and the nature without, or heaven and earth.

Accordingly, true men and women are those who have merged their thoughts and actions with the ever-changing transformations of the universe. At one with their spirit, such people act from their innermost being; they no longer deliberate or analyze about actions. They respond in the only way possible: the perfectly appropriate way.

When people act this way, they are acting true to their nature and, as such, are one with their nature, which is as real men and women. They are not acting morally or immorally, or as a particular kind of man or woman—for instance, a masculine version of a man or a feminine version of woman—or as good Christians or Muslims, or as secularists or fundamentalists; nor are they expected to conform. They are acting in harmony with their inner and outer worlds, without thought or inner conflict about how or why they should act one way or the other. It comes naturally through spirituality. That is our purpose in life, according to the spiritual traditions, to be a true man and a true woman, one with our true nature, which means bringing out our spirit.

Unfortunately, the paradigm of the West, its religious/secular view of reality, and the materialistic/artificial values it fosters have been eroding our purpose in life. At the same time, they have moved us away from our original nature and, in the process, away from our origins.

Because of this continual association with what is man-made as opposed to what is made naturally, we have come to identify ourselves in terms of our materialistic, physical, and social needs instead of in terms of our intrinsic nature and our spiritual roots.

This loss of our intrinsic nature, and the consequent inability to identify with our natural and spiritual connections, has led to a gradual decline in society in general and in the individual specifically, which is witnessed by the ever-increasing incidence of suicide, loss of direction, and overall sense of disconnection, meaninglessness, and unhappiness. It has also led to ever-increasing rates of cancer, diabetes, obesity, chronic illnesses, and incurable diseases.

This decline in society and in the individual has come about as a result of the rise of artificiality. Since we are living outside of nature, we have lost any personal connection to nature; thus, we are no longer able to identify ourselves as spiritual entities. This we can observe not through the acts of love, goodness, compassion, and tolerance, but through the acts of greed, violence, anger, lust, and attachment. Because we have been robbed of our true nature, which is our essence/spirit, we have lost any sense of virtue and virtuous living, the very qualities that distinguish us from other animals.

This spirit can only arise when conditions are right for it to arise, meaning when we are able to live and act in balance and in harmony with our inner and outer worlds—i.e., when we are in harmony with our spiritual and material worlds, or when we are in union with our environment and our original nature.

When these conditions exist, when we can act naturally—unaware of or unconcerned with society's view of reality and its artificial constructs, codes of conduct, and definitions of values—we will act appropriately at the time and in the exact moment, in relation to our conditions and our circumstances.

This is our natural state, and in this state we will manifest our natural patrimony and act accordingly, and our spirit will come out as it should. Thus, it is through the cultivation of self and the continuous study of nature that the principles of human nature are revealed, and we, as products of nature, should continuously seek to understand and live in harmony with the principles and laws of nature.

If we are able to live in accordance with the principles of nature and our own nature (our spirit), we will find ourselves free—free of the Dark Horse and the grip it has on us. In order to do that, however, we must begin to accept that nothing in the world is permanent, least of all ourselves.

When we are able to perceive life and reality this way—that nothing is permanent but in a constant state of change—we will come to understand that there is no absolute good or bad about the things in the world; nor is there an absolute entity, a *real* me, observing the things in the world. Everything is subject to change, including our perception of truth and reality. It depends entirely on *who* is looking, *when*, and *how* one is looking at things.

Both life and death arise from the mind and exist within the mind. The human mind is the chief of all events and all situations, and reality is relative to its interpretation. What is true and right today may be wrong and untrue tomorrow.

It is the human mind that processes the ability to think and gives life a meaning and a value; and it is the human mind that processes the ability to feel, which leads us to suicide and takes away any meaning and value in life.

The way we perceive and understand things around us happens in the mind. So it is imperative that we take care of and get control over our minds and come to understand that the ultimate explanations for all things are not always fully understood.

If we could come to see the nature of opposing values and phenomena as relative to the other and complementary—not as absolutes, but as related to and connected to others—we would be making a quantum leap forward.

If, on the other hand, we continue riding the Dark Horse and living with artificial and materialistic ways of seeing values and phenomena—by dividing and separating, exploiting and conquering, seeing everything as outside of us and as an adversary, fighting against others, fighting against nature, and fighting against ourselves—there will never be peace and harmony. We cannot see the big picture, which is only seen by looking at the whole, so we will continue to steadily decline.

The story of the fall of humankind comes about because of the realization or the objectification of the soul's Dark Horse. Once on earth, the soul is disconnected from its origins, the heavenly source. Without feeling connected to what is above, people come to think only in terms of what is below in this life.

As a result, humanity loses a sense of overall purpose and meaning, and thus loses itself in the material world and in the senses of self-indulgence and pleasure. The ego and its desires become the object of one's life instead of liberating oneself from them. The universal lack of spiritual fulfillment causes this fall of humankind.

People feel a sense of void all their lives because of this lack of spiritual fulfillment. No matter how much life brings their way, they still feel something is missing. To fill the void, they turn to obtaining worldly objects and beings as a means of doing so. The key is the perception of emptiness that is felt within and the need to fill it.

Now, instead of striving to return to the spiritual world, the soul is incarcerated in this material world and in the world of desire and illusion, in which it no longer has any recollection of where it came from, why it is here, and where it belongs. Basically, the soul no longer sees the big picture and no longer recalls any eternal ideals, or world of spirit, or what it should be striving for.

In this world, when the Dark Horse gains the upper hand, which it does by seeing the material world as the ultimate reality, the soul loses touch with the other world. Instead it falls in love with and becomes fascinated by the body and the body's pleasures, passions, and desires. Eventually the soul no longer has any reference to the world of spirit and comes to believe that truth exists only in bodily form, which a person may touch, see, and taste with his or her senses.

The soul becomes wedded to the senses of the body and uses them for the purposes of fulfilling all its desires and cravings. Fulfilling the body's desires becomes the aim in life, not pursuing the divine or spirit world. There is no end to these desires and cravings until the soul is able to purify itself and return to its old place in the company of gods.

It is only through the spirit, the higher self—or what Plato called the White Horse—that a soul can overcome such desires and recollect those things that it had once experienced in the spirit realm. This cannot happen in the mind. On the contrary, seeing things only through the mind and the senses will blind people to their true nature and origin.

Therefore, those who want to find the spirit realm must first find liberation from the ego—and the Dark Horse—and awaken the spirit. To do this, however, one must be able to gain control over one's senses; only then will one be able to resurrect his or her spirit form the land of illusions and dismount from the Dark Horse.

Once an individual gets off the Dark Horse and is in the company of the spirit, even for just a second, he or she can never be satisfied with the body and its pleasures again; nor can he or she associate with those who are obsessed with the material world and all its illusions. At this point, one turns his or her craving away from pleasure to the spiritual and is fixed on returning to the world he or she saw previously, even if for a second. The person desperately wants to get back on the White Horse and go to where he or she once again can pass into the world of purity, eternity, and immortality. He or she wants to go home. But the spirit needs to grow back its wings, and it needs help from nature to do that.

The key question to ask is how we are going to live our lives? *How* is the key word. Are we going to help the spirit grow back its wings, or are we going to pursue the life that gives us pleasure, security, and illusions, which is the way of the Dark Horse? Are we going to follow the spiritual path, or are we going to follow the material path?

The quest is neither in defining reality nor in defining truth; nor is it in looking for a purpose. The quest is in trying to answer how we are going to live life and how we are going to experience it deeply.

For this to happen, for us to learn the how, we must first be in a certain state that allows the answer to come—a state that naturally precludes the unnatural, artificial, and superficial from entering; a state of concentration; and a state of one-pointedness and nonduality.

That state can never come to those who are living materialistic and dualistic lives. It can never come to those who are ruled by the Dark Horse, with all its sensual desires, distractions, and illusions. It can never come to those who are smitten by the material world and its illusions.

That state can only come to those who are sincere and respectful, quiet and still—to those who are reverent and have a wholehearted commitment that enables them to reach the highest level of purity, tranquility, and harmony.

It cannot come to those who are living in the world of artificiality and man-made contrivances and illusions, but to those who are living natural, spontaneous lives and are one with nature. With spirit, we can enter into that state, a state of wisdom and intuition, and finally turn away from the illusory world of body and mind; we can begin to focus our attention on the spirit world. At this time, when we are not seeing with our eyes like others, not acting through our senses like others, and not riding on the Dark Horse like others, we are living with our being. We are transformed, and we begin to see things through the eye of our soul, or the third eye.

So the ultimate goal in life is not to live for and feed the desires of the body and the mind, according to the creed of the paradigm of the West. Instead it is to live for and feed the spirit and to begin to pierce through the surface of things, which we understand with our senses, and to penetrate to a deeper level of understanding, which is the true and underlying reality of nature. And we can only do this by first awakening the spirit.

We are not going to awaken the spirit by pretending that we are in the business of fixing a machine, with a "ghost" running the machine, and all we have to do is define the different systems and how they function to make it right. It's not just about energy and matter and how they affect each other in a three-dimensional reality.

We cannot study human and social life by simply studying its material and energetic components. Life exists within a relationship of many parts to the whole and the whole to many parts. The key is balance. When the elements of nature are in balance, life is harmonious and flourishes. When the balance of forces is upset, disaster comes.

Humans, who are sustained by the power of Earth and transformed by the power of the sun and the stars, cannot be separated from nature, no more than a tree can be separated from the earth, a bird can be separated from the sky, and a fish can be separated from the water.

We are no different from other creatures on this planet; indeed, we are nature in the form of people. What is good for nature is good for us, what is good for one is good for all, and what is good for the mind is good for the body.

Within this way of perceiving reality, the world is like a garden, and it is the role of each individual to cultivate life in the same way that one would take care of a garden. We cannot look at a wave independent of the ocean, and we cannot look at the ocean independent of the earth. And we cannot look at either independent of the atmosphere.

At the same time, we cannot look at the wave, the ocean, and the atmosphere independent of the planet and its relation to the solar system and the life force that circulates through everything and makes everything move, thereby influencing the weather—which affects the wave, the ocean, and the atmosphere.

Each and every thing on this earth is dependent on and influenced by a host of factors, none of which is the singular cause of anything else but is influenced by a confluence of other factors. Nothing happens in isolation; everything happens in relation to and dependent on other circumstances, conditions, elements, and factors. Thus, everything, including humanity, is relative to something else in space and time.

Like the links in a chain, if we hope to understand the essence of something, we must include all the links in that chain, all aspects of an entity. Its individual parts do not define the thing.

A chain is a chain because of its links. By the same token, a human is a human by virtue of his or her connection to the outer world and his or her inner world, or material world and spiritual world. This is what makes a human a human: the sum total of his or her links and connections.

But the moment we start separating people from their inner and outer environments, the moment we start isolating their feelings from their thoughts, their heart from their liver, their body from their mind and spirit, and their illness from their environment, we are no longer looking at humans as humans, but only as individual links in a chain.

Once we look only at the links and not at the whole, however, all contingent links are uncoupled and the originality, the essence/soul, is lost. We are not looking at a human anymore; that essence/soul has been lost by separating the human into parts and reducing him or her to complex molecular and genetic structures.

To bake a cake, one must bring together various ingredients and baking conditions. Take one away and substitute it with another, and we will not have a cake anymore. We will have something else instead, something that may look like a cake but is different because the necessary conditions for a cake to exist are no longer exact; the essence of the cake is no longer there.

To be a cake requires the exact conditions for "cakeness" to arise. When those specific conditions do not come into existence and are replaced by one or more factors—though we may have something that looks and feels like a cake—for all intents and purposes, it is no longer a cake because it no longer tastes like a cake. As a result, it has lost that which identifies it as a cake, and not only in its appearance but also in its taste.

By the same token, for a human to be a human, a host of factors must come together for one's "human-ness" to arise. Take one away, and the human will no longer manifest his or her true nature. Though one may still look and act like a human, it is only an appearance or an act in the same way that an altered cake only looks, smells, and feels like a cake.

But when you take a bite out of a cake that has been altered, or when you ask a human, who has been influenced by artifice and no longer lives according to the dictates of soul and virtue, to be human, you clearly realize that both are only facades because their essences are dormant, silenced, or have been artificially removed.

Essences/souls are eternal. There is no difference between a raindrop and the ocean, between life and death, or between spirit and humanity. By understanding the essence of life and the spirit of humankind, one can learn to follow the natural course closely and act according to the situation naturally and in harmony with the times.

Nature continuously undergoes the cycle of creation and destruction, and humans are no exception. Indeed, the ability to create and destroy defines the essence of nature; birth is the beginning of death, and death is the beginning of birth. Everything is forever undergoing a reversal and eventual transformation.

Instead of narrowing our focus on matter and reducing everything to its smallest component, we must begin to broaden our search and understanding of life. We should start reinterpreting life—and reality—in terms of functional relationships and processes, not only in terms of biological and chemical reactions. We should begin to broaden our horizons and see things in terms of unity and integration, not separation and division.

We must understand that life is nature and nature is life. They are mutually dependent, not mutually exclusive. Seen in this light, we will come to understand that nothing occurs outside of anything else;

everything is codependent, co-creative, and cogenerative—all within a naturally revolving and evolving cycle of patterns of energy, waves, and spirit.

We must put the spirit back into the body where it belongs and put the life force back into life, and we must once again start seeing that all things are connected and mutually dependent upon each other. Instead of a narrow focus on matter and energy, or religion and science, a broadening of vision about life, our interdependency, our connectivity, and the cohesion of phenomena is necessary.

From this way of unifying and integrating all aspects of life and living, a new vision will be born. This vision is based on a perception that clasps thought and feeling, mind and body, and spirit and matter, and looks at things holistically—in terms of unity, not division, and wholeness, not the narrow confines of parts. This vision will revolutionize our way of looking at nature and ourselves and how they are so intricately related to each other.

It will also finally get us back to reconnecting with our spirit and our natural roots and away from the exclusively materialistic, artificial, and dualistic mentality that is precipitating humankind's fall. This is the big picture, and realizing and living it is The Way.

All beings, not only human beings, belong to this universal oneness, with no disparity and no distinction. When we realize this, the universal principle of oneness, we will finally be healthy. We will realize that once we are free to see reality for ourselves, we can become one with the world around us. And when we get off the Dark Horse and stop living the illusory life as propounded by the paradigm of the West, we can start living in harmony with our environment.

That is the alternative way, which is the only sustainable way to good health, wellness, happiness, and a spiritually fulfilling life and lifestyle. But in order to realize this way, we must first free ourselves of the Dark Horse and break away from the noise and clamor of our conditioning, which greatly disturbs the spirit.

About the Author

The royal family of Bhutan—a quiet, gentle, and spiritually unique and exotic country in the foothills of the Himalayas—bestowed the title of "lama" on Nicholas Packard. *Lama* means spiritual teacher, and that he is. In China his students call him "master," and that he is, too. How did this happen? How did this American man from the steel mills of Pittsburgh find himself with the titles "lama" and "master"?

His early gifts pointed to a life as a celebrated American athlete. As a teenager, he was a bright student and a star athlete in baseball, basketball, and golf. He was a natural. Professional scouts pursued him with eyes on him making a career in baseball, but that was not his destiny. The golden-boy luster and his boyhood dreams vanished overnight. An accident that resulted in a broken back, epileptic seizures, and the inability to walk moved him toward a drastically different life journey. Eventually he retrieved his mobility, but any concept of normality was lost to him. This was his first watershed of disillusionment.

Like other young adults in his generation, he still did the conventional things like getting a degree in philosophy and a postgraduate degree in international affairs at the University of Pittsburgh. Packard went to work at the Environmental Protection Agency in Washington after graduation and worked for the Peace Corps. He even became a playwright and took up residence on the Lower East Side of New York City to try to make it in the theater. Despite not living a particularly normal life, he still entertained aspirations and goals of personal success in the material world.

An Italian producer recognized Packard's talent as a playwright in New York and asked him to come to Italy to produce his plays. Packard obliged. But it took longer than expected to produce them, so in order to stay longer, Packard took a job writing for the pharmaceutical industry as it began its ascent to power, money, and international influence and importance.

Eventually his plays were produced to great fanfare, and his career in the pharmaceutical industry was equally successful. Having learned to speak Italian fluently, he even directed plays in Italian. He was a great success. Packard was living a dream. He had everything, but something was amiss. It didn't mean anything to him, not being with the narcissists of show business or the power mongers of the corporate world.

He had discovered firsthand how empty and deceptive both businesses were, and he could no longer live with himself after discovering what was really going on inside both industries. With that came his second watershed of disillusionment. But this time around he was no longer able to adapt, so he decided to throw caution—and any semblance of normality—to the wind and left it all. He left for India, never to return to his comfortable life in Italy or the West. He left his apartment—and all his books, clothes, and belongings, not to mention his money and fame—and the conventional life.

He lived in the mountains of India for ten years. His experiences there were extraordinary for personal transformation. Vedic astrologers predicted he would become a healer. He scoffed in disbelief but found himself in situations where his energy-light body opened up to extreme experiences of Kundalini forces. That was just the beginning, but his rational mind could not accept this lifestyle, and it prevented him from healing. His gifts were too compelling and intense though, and the needs of the sick and dying were just too great, so eventually he relented and became a healer in India, just as predicted.

Packard's healing gifts led him from the mountains of India to the mountains of China. For another ten years, he learned from Gao Yang Meng, Yongqiu Xiao, and Lizhong Chen, strict and unyielding grand masters of China. He was a Westerner who, year after year, submitted to rigorous training in traditional Chinese medicine and its holistic healing principles, as well as the practice of Tai Chi and Qigong. All the while he continued to have unusual and inexplicable experiences allowing him to go deeper into his phenomenal healing gifts.

After thirty years of living in the East—immersed in the way of the Tao in India, China, Tibet, Bhutan, and Thailand—Packard has come to believe that *The I Ching",* feng shui, the Chinese discovery of qi, and the universal principles of yin and yang are perhaps the greatest contributions the Chinese have made to world civilization. Indeed, they actually map out and explain the order of the universe. His success in healing partly comes from his formidable training and ability to combine Buddhist, Hindu, and Chinese principles of this ancient wisdom, allowing him to glean the "missing" link for humanity. The other part is too mysterious to explain – and too sacred to put into words.

Printed in Great Britain
by Amazon